Copyright 2011

Success Strategies for Technology Management

This is dedicated to all my professional
friendships — for their contributions to
my great education and wonderful
experiences.
There are too many of you to list.
You know who you are.

My special thanks and appreciation go
to Anthony, Mark and Richard for their
enlightened input and to my editor
Benjamin.
Thanks to Marie for the cover photo.
Thanks to Susan for her moral support.

TABLE OF CONTENTS

Introduction

Leadership skills are not mysterious and can be learned. You may already possess the skills required and may not realize it. There are many people that have excellent leadership skills, but refuse to exercise them for personal reasons. There is nothing wrong with that—in fact; part of being a good Leader involves your willingness to sacrifice for others. Sacrifice is giving up something good for something better. The combination of sacrifice, commitment, courage, and risk are not part of everyone's personal constitution. If you cannot find happiness or contentment in sacrifice for others, then leadership is not the correct path for you. If you lack the courage to take a risk, and the audacity to be right when you know that you are right, then leadership is not the correct path for you. Utilizing the lessons outlined in this writing will help you to be more successful and a happier person, eventually bringing you additional income as you become a most desirable member in your organization.

In the beginning of my career in Information Technology (IT), I never viewed myself as a Leader, but always as a worker. I have come to find that leaders are workers also, albeit in a different sense. The requirements for engineers are very clear—gaps in knowledge are usually easy to see, and can be addressed through books, tutorial or instructional classes. Management is a disciplined profession. Effective leadership requires many of those management skills, but it is more abstract and intangible. Primarily, it is the compassion to understand people in the most basic sense, the ability to form a vision, and the courage to execute said vision, that are all required for great leadership.

I first began realizing my leadership potential just a few years into my career, performing project work with leadership requirements, without a leadership title. Personal interaction with peers began to improve to a state that was clearly more productive. The fact that I was not officially recognized as a Leader made it much more comfortable for me to ask people to do things for me to optimize each project's chances for success. I learned how to gain the support of smart engineers without the use of authority.

After learning the basics of what works and what doesn't work, I began to see productive results. Not only were the results productive, but people started to request participation on my project teams. They began to ask if they could help, and wanted to know what they could do. There were other Project Managers that were as smart as, or smarter than me, but they tended to demand support as if it was their right. Technology engineers don't react well to that sort of entitlement, and they respond accordingly.

My bosses started to notice the magnitude of my successes. Helping them look good incented them to reward me—in small ways, initially (e.g.; pats on the back), and then in more tangible ways:

- Trade show attendance

- Exotic business travel
- Approvals for large purchases
- Staff retention
- Better assignments
- Excellent performance reviews
- Pay increases
- Large bonuses
- Stock options

Sharing credit for success with those that help to realize it, and ensuring that credit is shared through rewards, is the correct way to establish respect and build relationships. During a stint as a Project Manager, I started to think about my role and the possibility of becoming a staff Manager.

Taking a risk and accepting additional responsibility outside of my current organization was a career catalyst. I was moderately successful at first, and then more successful. The environment was that of IT Infrastructure, so it was not strange to me, but it was very demanding and not at all easy. Personalities in my organization were challenging, and the technical environment was very unstable. I approached each situation with an open mind, making sure to keep my personal feelings in check.

As I became more successful, improving my leadership skills through a combination of company—sponsored education and trial—and—error, life improved. At first, I struggled and did not enjoy my work, but soon enough, successes started to compound upon successes. It took about one year, but I began to leave the office at the end of the day energized, with a smile on my face and a hop in my step. I no longer viewed the job as work, but as an opportunity—or a string of opportunities—to accomplish great things. Possibilities were everywhere, and were restricted only by my mind. My responsibilities expanded further as I was asked to manage additional areas and staff. I really loved it.

Experiences as an IT Architect Consultant and as a Pre-Sales Systems Engineer provide insight from the vendor side of deals. I could see the partnership opportunities from both perspectives.

Because of my professional education and real world experiences, I confidently assert myself as being qualified to write this. I am eager to share my experiences and opinions and offer this writing to IT professionals.

It is my intention to capture what I have learned, and to share it with you to assist you in finding and sustaining success and happiness. Success is a cooperative effort, and you are not alone. You will find me emphasizing *team* throughout this writing. You will also find many quotes and examples from famous leaders throughout the text; they were selected for their relevance and truthfulness as they pertain to the opinions being shared.

I sincerely believe that every dark cloud has a silver lining, but unless you look for it, you will probably never see it. We need to search relentlessly for that silver lining.

I sincerely believe in these writings, and I have found success through the practice of these beliefs. This book is purposefully brief to encourage full reading. It will not take long to complete this, and the rewards can be of tremendous benefit to your career.

Have fun. Take notes. Practice what you read. See what works for you. Improve where you can. Someday, perhaps you can create something similar that encourages others to become happy and successful Leaders.

Until you develop the qualities of a Leader—on fire with an inspiring vision, living by noble principles, genuinely caring for others and dedicated to brutal honesty in all things—you're as handicapped in your pursuit of a better life as a three—legged horse would be at the Kentucky Derby.

— Dr. Symeon Rodger

Chapter 1

Your Role in the Organization

Regardless of your role in an organization, management and leadership are always choices. One has to be committed; management and leadership do not work without each other. Leaders must manage, and Managers must often lead.

Know your position. Know the limitations of your position. Know your personal limits. Most of all, know the opportunities available to you in your position—there are probably more than you realize. Seize the opportunities that bring the most value first and can be completed relatively quickly.

Always be honest, and lead by example. There is no faking character. Your true character is reflected by how you act when no one is watching. *Live what you preach.* As I tell my older son: *Show* your younger brother what an important responsibility it is to collect and take the garbage out twice a week. Allow him to see you working and doing a good job for the family. If you want your younger brother to enthusiastically help you and one day assume your duties, then *lead by example.*

[13]

This method can be effective in the workplace as well. In all situations, honesty should triumph, and the virtues of the job should be admitted openly.

For example:

Several years ago, I was at work very late with an engineer, troubleshooting an elusive problem, recreating the scenario, and interpreting the results again and again.

During a silent period around midnight, I looked at him and, smiling, said, "This really sucks, doesn't it?" He smirked and agreed. It effectively communicated to him that I was in this mess with him, sharing his feelings, and that I was confident that we would get out of this together. Soon after, we were able to correct the problem and go home. The next day, being in on time, I asked him if he wanted to go home at lunchtime on that day, or wait until Friday to go home at lunchtime. He was very happy, and selected Friday. As the Manager, I had the power to allow this to happen, so why not do it? It made this team member happy, and it set an example for other members of the team, who would now be more willing to work late when necessary.

I, however, enjoyed no such reward. Remember to sacrifice for success. My reward was the loyalty of this valued team member and the promise of his future loyalty, commitment and success.

Technology can be a blessing or a curse. Often, technology will provide ninety—nine solutions to solve a given problem in IT, and all of these solutions may work, but only two or three of them will work ideally. Which solution is best—suited for your environment should be determined on the basis of advice from your technical team, but the decision itself rests entirely with the leader.

For these reasons, surrounding yourself with skilled and talented individuals is crucial to your success. You cannot find all of the answers yourself, no matter how good you are. It is fruitless to surround yourself with technically competent people that do not share your values and ethics, because you will need these people to be truthful—to know when to alert you of any development that you might not endorse—and must trust in them.

Initiate the process of *Critical Thinking*. Critical thinking involves the identification of issue(s), of each variable contributing to the current situation, and of all possible variables and actions that could change the situation to everyone's benefit. You must rely on your team to help you identify all variables.

Sometimes, it is what it is. You must change what you can, but you must also be able to know what is beyond your power to change. A condition being *it is what it is* indicates that you should accept the situation at face value and not read some deeper explanation or significance into it. In every case, you will have to make the best of the situation that has presented itself to you. Never try to force an improbable success.

On a project team for a prominent client, the client's representative was demanding implementation in three days. The Project Manager reluctantly informed her that influences outside his control rendered such an outcome impossible. The customer became angered, and threatened to escalate the issue. The Project Manager stood firm, however, and stated simply that if we forced implementation within three days, success would be very unlikely.

Success was critical for the project team and for the customer. To force implementation under the existing circumstances would have been irresponsible and unwise. Sometimes it is what it is. Forcing it to be something that it's not is not a helpful or appropriate decision. The Project Manager wisely alerted his Managers of the situation and of the client's feelings.

Try always to remember the Serenity Prayer:
God, grant me the serenity to accept the things I cannot change,
Courage to change the things I can, and wisdom to know the difference.

Seek, find, and seize opportunities. Opportunity is always present. Find it and spread the good word. Others will see you transform an undesirable situation into an opportunity, and they will respect you for it. This is another instance of leading by example, and another opportunity to gain respect.

Seek, find, and seize opportunities.

Collaborate with other Managers, because other IT Managers will be tremendous assets to your success. Nurture these peer relationships by sharing time and developing camaraderie. You will work with them often, and you will, at times, rely on their cooperation.

Lastly, even though IT is a cost center and you are expected to save wherever you can, *this is not your reason for being there.* Nor should saving money be your primary goal. You occupy your position in order to provide a service to the business that will allow them to do what they do in order to make money. There are many Managers that will compromise levels of service in order to trim expenses. This is absolutely the wrong approach—the company will never reward you, or respect you, for choosing to save a buck and cutting corners, risking their ability to conduct business.

The business will, however, be extremely grateful if you provide a reliable, high—performance service that provides a useful tool for them to excel in business. You need only justify your spending. It may sound difficult or intimidating, but you will see how simple it can be.

Aim to provide the best service that you can, and then negotiate for the best price that you can get. Get competitive bids from different sources. Be thorough and honest. Show your character. You will be rewarded for providing such a service. You will likely never be rewarded for saving a buck by compromising service levels, and you could find yourself looking for another employer.

It is usually beneficial to maintain a diverse vendor environment (e.g., two server manufacturers, two or more telecommunications carriers). This approach will help to keep vendors on their best behavior, making them less likely to deliver an inferior product or service. Price negotiation is easily performed from this position as well. Avoid single vendor solutions where possible. Even a low, volume pricing structure does not outweigh the benefits provided by multiple providers. You should always respect the vendors that you bring into your company. Never arrogantly abuse them or take advantage of the precariousness of their sales to your company.

When multiple vendors for similar solutions are not available, you may have to pay a bit more for their no—bid service, but you must still try to negotiate the best price that they can give you.

Chapter 2

Manager, Leader, or Both?

Management is about arranging and telling. Leadership is about nurturing and enhancing.

—Thomas J. Peters

To be a great Manager and Leader, the following points should be practiced:

1. Your attitude, behavior, and sense of worth in both yourself and others all have a powerful effect on your success as a leader. Always be positive and optimistic, because every cloud has a silver lining, and it's up to you to find it.

2. Be direct and drive straight to the issue at hand, but not in such a way that might hurt the person responsible. No one likes to be told that they are wrong, so it is wise to avoid doing so. Often, to hurt someone by being critical is unavoidable. Those instances call for a positive attitude, a lot of guts and authentic diplomacy. For example: *Even though it is now causing a problem, I can understand the factors that led to that decision and I may have done the same thing in your shoes.*

[19]

However, at this time, we need to move forward and seek a change or resolution that will free us from the current situation. Be yourself, and inject your own personality into these interactions.

Universally speaking, people are people. Everyone has some variation of these common feelings as found in a list created by John C. Maxwell*1:

1. Everybody Wants to Be Somebody
2. Nobody Cares How Much You Know until They Know how Much You Care
3. Everybody Needs Somebody
4. Everybody Can be Somebody when Somebody Understands and Believes in Them
5. Anybody that Helps Somebody Influences a Lot of Bodies!

Nobody wants to be challenged with the language and intentions of a good politician, and everybody despises a liar. Use diplomacy and tact, and never lie. Build trust, for it is crucial to leadership. Don't be afraid to appear vulnerable.

We trust people we believe are real and human (i.e.; imperfect and flawed)—just like us. So, allow others a glimpse of your vulnerabilities (honest and genuine, and not fabricated). This enables them to relate to you on a more basic, human level, as opposed to your being an aloof dictator.

*1. Maxwell, John Calvin. *John Maxwell's Ten Leadership Keys: Understanding People*, Retrieved June 6, 2011 from
http://selfimprovement.info—just—for—u.com/blogger/communication—skills/john—maxwell%E2%80%99s—ten—leadership—keys—understanding—people/

The world is not a perfect place and as a Leader working with customers, be they internal or external, you will encounter occasions in which the best course of action will include stretching the truth a bit. Do not be afraid to occasionally break your own rules. If you find yourself cornered and feel you absolutely have to lie about something you were committed to do, but did not, the prudent action you must take is to 'make it the truth' as soon as you possibly can. You must remain committed to the truth. By the close of business, or as soon as possible, your lie must become the truth. Do this on extreme and desperate occasions only. Do not make it a habit, because you will eventually get caught and lose several degrees of respect and credibility. It can take you a long time to recover your reputation after a slip like this is seen by your customers as your standard or default mode of operation.

If you find you are incapable of quickly making your lie the truth, own up to it immediately, explaining to the party you had committed to, that circumstances have created a delay or are preventing you from completing the commitment as promised. Assume ownership and offer alternate actions that may be considered less than optimal, but acceptable. Do not procrastinate, because time will only exacerbate the lie and more seriously damage your reputation. Commit to re-double your efforts to achieve the new goal as soon as possible.

———————————

I'm sure you have heard this before, but it bears repeating: A Leader is a visionary, so the details will be left to the talented, creative minds that they set to the task. Leaders don't sweat details—they delegate and trust in a satisfactory completion. That is why it is important for leaders to surround themselves with talented people that share their values.

Background, age, ethnicity, education, and experience will vary from person to person, and selection should not be based on any of these attributes alone. When evaluating a team, the Leader must be able to recognize voids in skill sets so that actions can be taken to address them, either by education or with help from a mentor who is a Subject—Matter Expert (SME).

Leaders can visualize their future. They become passionate about achieving the vision until they are living and breathing it. They keep the vision in their minds and hearts — truly loving it. Passion is the intangible thing that will often get you through when everything else fails. The love and passion becomes contagious, and others want to follow— even individuals not on your team. Being a team member becomes desirable, valued, and even coveted. Once you have started building your team, you must trust in them to execute your vision. Trust in your team is part of the teambuilding process.

Don't be too concerned with having deep technical understanding. Managers and leaders don't need to have a deep understanding of any technology because they are surrounding themselves with talented people who do. These individuals should be ethical, have a strong work ethic, and be loyal, talented, and intelligent. It sounds like a tall order, but is not a rare find under good leadership. Make your people aware of your expectations.

We don't always pick the people around us; in these cases, we must help them to develop into what we need, or remove them.

Passion often separates the Leaders from the Managers. Remember: Managers must often lead, and leaders must manage to some degree. Without management skills, a Leader is likely to fail. Conversely, without basic leadership skills, a manager will be hard pressed to inspire anybody. Both are important components.

Your team must become your family—trusted and loved. My wife told me that I treated my work team like my family. I replied that the difference was that my kids at work do what I say. Leaders must be happy to always put the team's needs ahead of their own—to sacrifice themselves. Find out what is important to each team member. A good example of this is to determine the family status of each individual. Learn the names of spouses and even children. Write the names down and memorize them. When you have to phone them at their house and you can greet their spouse by name, it demonstrates that you care and you respect that person's family. Make a note of birth days and acknowledge the days when they come around each year. Apply this insight wherever possible. Demonstrate sincere empathy. Show respect to gain respect.

Great leaders are generally good, friendly people whom you would like to have as your friend.

[23]

- Be friendly, but stay strong.
- Be consistent in your actions and words.
- Do not be a mystery to your team. You require trust. Mystery will not promote trust, but distrust. Nothing will destroy a team quicker than a lack of trust in the Leader.

Great leaders are champions of their own lives. They know who they are, what they stand for, and where they are going. For this reason, and because they know these things to be absolutely true, they are capable of leading others. You cannot ask others to be complete and thorough, and expect them to comply, if your own life is in disarray. Therefore, you must believe in yourself and your abilities first.

By the same token, however, these leadership attributes can lead to overconfidence, arrogance, and ill feelings from other Managers and business leaders. You should be striving for respect and acceptance. Watch yourself through the eyes of others. Aim to never be arrogant, but always to be worthy of respect.

Always be worthy of respect.

As you establish self—confidence (it takes time and experience), find ways to build confidence in your people. You will need to challenge individuals to extend themselves farther than they are accustomed to going—get beyond their comfort zone. The challenge may be technical in nature, or it may involve pairing workers that do not like each other. Encourage individuals to reach for greater accomplishments, explaining that you have a need and that you can think of no one better qualified to fulfill it. It is sometimes a good strategy to pair high performers with others that need help to become the high performers that you want them to become. Be honest and sincere. It will help them, and thus, help you.

You may want to appeal directly to their pride by affirming how important they are to the success of the organization—how you depend on them. Make it personal.

No try. Do or Do not. There is no try.

—Yoda

Confidence is a fragile thing, so be careful not to crush it with a poorly placed word. Never tell someone that they are "wrong". What a powerful, damaging word. Nobody likes to be wrong—to fail. Instead, clarify the options and the value of each, and where things can be done more effectively. Let them know at the same time how much you value their input and how important they are to the team.

There was an episode where my team was working on a failed hardware component, leaving the business to use an alternative system that left them vulnerable to outage and with slower transaction times. The hardware vendor was sending a replacement part via courier. The entire staff was aware the part was coming, but one of my ace engineers was in charge of the repair and responsible for the job. That afternoon, between meetings, I decided to check with him on the status of the repair. He proceeded to tell me that the part had arrived almost an hour ago, but no one was taking any action with it. He was upset that he alone was responsible, and he did not feel this was his problem alone. Even though I was shocked by this response, I apologized for not making myself clearer earlier. I carefully explained to him that I counted on him for this, making it personal, because I felt he was my best hope for resolving this situation as quickly as possible. I sympathized by letting him know I understood his frustrations with the team, and that we would discuss this at a later time. However, I made it clear that serving the business was our primary mission and that is what we needed to do—immediately. Feeling that I understood the situation and having shown that I appreciated his value, he hurriedly got to work on the problem and we were back to normal operation by evening.

In retrospect, candor and honesty were invaluable in motivating this top-notch engineer to resolve the issues. My sympathy, words, and feelings not only motivated him, but also boosted his morale, enhancing both his self-respect and his respect for me. I was able to place myself in his position demonstrating empathy. He was told, in not so many words, that he was the linchpin to our success in this situation. The team was later apprised of their part in this dynamic. Above all, though, the emphasis was on our mission, with the entire team's united effort necessary to pull together to get it done.

Apathy is an important responsibility for leaders of teams. Leaders must create buy-in and build consensus around ideas. You must understand your team's point of view to understand how they will respond to new ideas. Consequently, the leadership trait of apathy helps make leaders more successful.

Distribute your attentions evenly and wisely. Be positive and supportive to all. A Leader cannot afford to play favorites, but high—performance contributors need proper compensation, and are good candidates for mentoring.

Always recognize and reward good performance to the appropriate level. A lack of recognition discourages future efforts. A lack of reward serves as disapproval. Set an example for the rest of the team to see. If criticism is necessary, it must be positive and constructive—never degrading.

Bonus time is a good time to recognize high—performance contributors. For the distribution of bonuses, use one simple guideline: think of the people whose absence or departure would hurt you most, and reward them with the largest bonus. Usually, loyalty will be strengthened, which is your intention. Should other team members complain about their bonuses, carefully explain what they must do in order to attain what they desire, always thinking to yourself that any more bonus money for them, has to be taken away from your high performing people. It will help if you create a list of goals for the individual. If your organization does not have bonuses at this level, use merit increases in a similar fashion.

Mangers are vital to all organizations. Checklists, milestones, budgets, etc. are all tools of great Managers. The Manager must be organized and be aware of all the tasks they are responsible for, maintain project timelines and anticipate milestones while at the same time, have a solid knowledge of all the activities taking place in their organization at any given time, and report status at any time. A Manager budgets effectively. A strong work ethic is required for success.

Managers have to adopt leadership traits in order to manage successfully, and should demonstrate leadership potential while functioning in the Manager position.

Now, about your technical ideas: Your ideas must always have substantial support from *at least* two reputable sources. These could be as specific as past successes, or as general as magazine features/tests. Reference the supporting sources in your proposal. Validate the idea with your technical team before proposing. Gather feedback regarding your ideas and actions. Members of your team and others will have opinions about what you are doing, and you must listen attentively and be sincerely interested. You don't always have to adjust your strategy based on their input, and you will know how to approach it with different people; what is important to them is how your leadership will affect them. Not everyone will agree all of the time.

In one case, after receiving a request from an executive, I hired a consultant to review my plans and provide critical comments. The consultant reviewed my plans for infrastructure changes and a meeting was scheduled to review his interpretations and suggestions. The team was familiar with the plans, participated in their development and actively participated in the review sessions with the consultant SME. The plan was not modified, but after hearing what he found difficult to understand, the methods in which the proposal was written and presented to executives was modified in order to help me simplify it so that I could focus on pitching the considerable investment being requested.

No matter what you decide to do, all of your team must be in agreement. Once they have participated in the idea process, they will acquire some sense of ownership and pride for the idea and proposal that will only grow through its implementation.

Through these honest and sincere actions, you are communicating to your staff that *you are important to me; I value your expertise and commitment.* Mutual respect is being built with honesty and sincerity.

Remember this: Whoever sows sparingly will also reap sparingly, and whoever sows generously will also reap generously.
— 2 Corinthians 9:6-8

In life, there are givers and takers. Givers give cheerfully of whatever they have—even if it is only friendship, encouragement, and service—and always reap a reward that enriches them as people. Takers—who are always on the take, to see what they can get for themselves—will always be impoverished as persons, no matter how materially wealthy they become. Give generously.

Managers and Leaders are required to both know and understand their areas in enough detail to gain respect within the organization, and to make decisions appropriate to their positions. As a Leader, you must add value to the business. Occasionally, leaders will make decisions that worsen situations. Sometimes, in spite of best efforts, dedication, skills, and conduct, the outcome is not always best—or, at least, what we had planned.

Make sure to always stand by your decisions, and to own up to your missteps (i.e., failures) just as passionately as you stand up for your successes. Have integrity in everything that you say and do. Responsibility always stops with the leader. A Leader does not have the luxury to deflect blame for failures. Assuming responsibility for your decisions, good or bad, is essential to leadership.

You are likely a Manager and a Leader. Personal attributes are very similar, but Leaders require more from their team(s).

Essential attributes/skills are (in no particular order):
- Honesty/Integrity
- Loyalty
- Confidence/Faith
- Respect, Apathy & Trust
- Organized
- Loyalty
- Technical insight
- Relaxer/De—stressor

Organizational skills and a solid work ethic are additional prerequisites for these positions.

If you have Managers that are adept with the tools of the position, let them see that you know the demands of their workload (i.e., show empathy), and that you are happy with their work (i.e., demonstrate respect and appreciation). If they are not using a tool that you would like for them to use, suggest it. Be tactful. Offer to purchase the tool for them. Explain your reasoning, and explain the ways in which you feel that it could assist them and the entire team. When they are good, let them know it.

Leadership will be measured by your contribution to the business. Don't be afraid to take calculated risks in order to enhance the business. We are all engaged in risk management everyday for every decision.

Good leadership requires some risk. Taking risks requires genuine courage. You cannot have genuine courage without confidence. You must have both courage and confidence in yourself and your team to take risks. Consider that, at times, the right decision is not the most popular; a good Leader must have the courage to choose it anyway. Say, for instance, that you will have to propose a technology that is not preferred by peers or superiors, due to preconceived ideas that they harbor about the technology or the reputation of the vendor.

For example:

A smaller vendor's high—performance UNIX server technology was proposed for technical reasons, while the vendor preferred by executives was the large, incumbent vendor who was arguably not as well—versed in newer technologies. Proposing the newer, unpopular vendor required courage that was supported by published testing and case studies. In the final hours, a third vendor was selected that met the needs of all parties. The vendor was comfortably large, established, and an industry—wide performance Leader who had offered substantial incentives for the company to switch from the existing vendor. These incentives were not being offered by the originally proposed high—performance vendor. The compromises were acceptable to all, and implementation proceeded successfully.

Take intelligent risks that have adequate technical and financial support. Even when you are confident your point of view is correct, and there is substantial supporting evidence, proposing a solution that counters executive wishes is a slippery slope that requires extra due diligence and preparation. When evidence has been presented and executives still appear unwilling to consider your proposed alternative, it is prudent to give up on your proposal. Especially if the solution desired by the executive

- *Be humble, seek, and accept criticism*
- *Acknowledge and be grateful for all advice*
- *Do not command conformity*

Leadership is not a right, but a privilege.

can be made to work effectively with some extra effort from you and the vendor. In those cases it will be best to throw up the white flag and make amends with your opponents. There is no shame in accepting defeat and playing it smarter and safer.

The example above illustrates when you have the courage to propose what is best, even if you don't get exactly what you want, you will be better off for showing the courage to propose the unpopular, but more promising solution. Many times you will find that compromise, as in this example, is the best course — for you, for your boss, for the company.

Upon presenting a proposal, risks require courage and should have contingencies. Every change has risk. Contingencies build safety into a risky proposition. Be ready to share your contingency ideas with company leaders in a way they can easily understand, and be prepared to execute in the event they are required. If there are no viable contingencies, the business needs to be aware so they understand their exposure and what action can be taken to minimize damage to the business. Lack of viable contingencies could be the death of your proposal, but the death of your proposal may be best for the company and your career.

Be humble, seek, and accept criticism. Acknowledge and be grateful for all advice. Leadership is not a right, but a privilege. Treat it as such and do not demand conformity.

Finally, your personal presentation is often greatly underestimated. Think and look positive and optimistic. You want to be seen as a respected Leader and a contributor. Dress and speak the part. Business environments vary today more than ever, to the point where it is no longer obvious how to dress.

Given that, the attire of a Leader and the ability to precisely articulate your thoughts in an educated manner are important. It's alright to pause for a few seconds to think about your response before speaking. In a business environment, simple, concise speech—delivered at a moderate pace—is preferred. By observing executive leadership in your environment, you will be able to determine how you should dress. It is a fact, whether you like it or not: neat, attractive people garner more respect and receive more opportunities than do sloppy, disheveled people. You need to exude self—confidence, and your appearance is the first step toward your doing so, followed closely by your speech.

Articulate your ideas and thoughts simply, concisely, and clearly. Avoid the so—called *$10 words* that have a tendency to make good Managers look silly. Avoid terms like *yup*, *ain't*, and most street slang. Simple, intelligent speech is ideal, spoken at a comfortable rate. There are many publications from reputable authors that offer advice and assistance on the subject of articulation and speaking. The way that you speak shows your level of education as well as comfort, and can impact both the level of respect that you receive and the approval rate of your proposals.

Listening is often more valuable than speaking. Teach yourself the patience to listen when you feel like talking. Listen to the opinions of the talented people around you, evaluate their input, and then make your decision.

We have two ears, two eyes, and one mouth. We should try to keep that ratio in perspective by listening and watching at least twice as often as we speak.

Sometimes one creates a dynamic impression by saying something, and sometimes one creates as significant an impression by remaining silent.

—Dalai Lama

When you do speak, talk about subjects you know, and know well. If you are uncertain, it's alright to say so with a commitment to research deeper when you can. If the subject is completely foreign to you, it is best to remain silent. If asked, be honest. These traits have been observed in others at early stages in my career—some that spoke constantly, and others that listened intently before speaking; people that flat—out lied or others that liked to stretch the truth a bit. I found that, even when listeners didn't win a given battle, they usually ended up winning the war. To win the war, you need to be observant (watching), respectful (listening), and intelligent (learning), using the time necessary to obtain the input that will empower you to make the correct choices.

Practice listening and watching at least twice as often as you speak.

It is alright to communicate your own personal opinions on a subject. In most of these situations, the wisest course is to point out that this is your personal opinion. Your listener will appreciate your acknowledgment and will typically respect your opinion (but not always agree).

[35]

Work on your physical appearance. A tidy, clean, ordered appearance can provide self confidence. Physical fitness adds tremendously to your appearance and also builds self confidence. Join a gym and visit regularly, building stamina, strength and confidence with each visit.

This seems simple, but don't be rude or obnoxious. Mind your manners, because being polite and accommodating will get you more than being rude and obnoxious every time. Chew with your mouth closed. Don't interrupt unless you excuse yourself first and have something relevant to say. Hold the door for others. When you step into an occupied elevator, offer a greeting ("good morning"). Manners are generally acquired and developed in childhood, but may need refreshing before you can be accepted as a leader. Good manners won't be discussed in any more detail here, but I would like to provide an example of how being nice, using good manners, and having courteous, professional consideration can help you meet your goals.

Early in my career, I was asked to design an infrastructure to support financial reporting from several offices in South America. Immediately, I borrowed Spanish—language educational tapes from the Travel Department. I spent a couple dozen hours listening to and learning Spanish. I even purchased a Spanish newspaper to improve my reading and comprehension skills. The tapes taught me how to speak more quickly than my college professor who emphasized proper grammar. I was able to learn much in just a few weeks. The business trips to cities in South America came up quickly, so my goal of speaking Spanish fluently before traveling had not been met. However, I attempted to use what I had learned. I found that business associates in South America were very appreciative that I was attempting to converse in their language, but once they realized I was struggling, they happily spoke English for me. Their English was far better than my Spanish. Even associates in Brazil demonstrated a great appreciation for my attempt to learn Spanish. The language in Brazil is Portuguese, but they were able to understand most Spanish. I found their ability to comprehend my Spanish was not important because they spoke English fluently. The fact that they understood I was trying to learn the Spanish language was enough for me to earn their respect and appreciation. The associate with whom I was traveling, who did not know Spanish or Portuguese, was also impressed and found that my grasp of Spanish, no matter how rudimentary, was adequate to speak with cab drivers and airline officials regarding basic instructions and flight questions. In Brazil, while taking us to the airport, the cab driver rambled off a long monologue in Portuguese. When I replied, "United Airlines", my American associate nearly fell off of his seat in surprise. He was that impressed, and said so. The gracious cooperation I received from local Managers was greatly appreciated, and continued through months of follow—up phone meetings.

The unexpected lesson I received is that people will appreciate you more when you try to make their job easier, even when you fail. Be nice and try to be accommodating.

By the time you have completed this writing, you should be able to differentiate between leadership and management and see that the personality traits for each position are mostly interchangeable. I have met Managers that couldn't lead, but I have not met a Leader who couldn't manage.

If your actions inspire others to dream more, learn more, do more and become more, you are a leader.

—John Quincy Adams

———————

Terms defined as used in this writing:

- **Confidence** — Knowledge of yourself and your profession; never doubting yourself, but always consulting with others, listening for input and making adjustments as appropriate.
- **Faith** — Belief in God, in people, and in yourself—delegate and be comfortable with both your team and the goodness of your people—believe in your ability to know right from wrong.
- **Honesty/Integrity** — Knowledge of your area and being consistently truthful and optimistic.
- **Loyalty** — Devotion to your team, your organization, and your leader.
- **Organized** — Efficiency in tracking of people, projects, and budgets, with an array of tools.
- **Relaxer** — A learned skill calming others; for handling stressful situations in which you can only observe, and must rely on others to resolve: *We can only do that which is within our power.*
- **Respect** — Thoughtful consideration for all others and for yourself.

- **ROI** (*Return on Investment*) — The amount of time required to recoup the initial cost of the proposed financial investment.

- **TCO** (*Total Cost of Ownership*) — The recurring expense of supporting a proposed solution.

- **Technically competent** — A deep understanding of not only the technologies in the area of responsibility, but also how those technologies impact the organization.

Chapter 3

Get Organized

Organization skills are typically greatly underestimated or greatly overestimated, and they require a delicate balance with other activities. People that possess great organization skills already know how critical they are. However, overdoing your organization skills leads to consumption of your valuable time. Areas that will suffer include team morale, project completion dates, future vision, family, etc. You can get so involved in being organized that the activities you are organizing never get done or get done poorly—just to satisfy your "to—do list".

There is always the danger for micro—management that should be avoided. Managers should not be concerned with every minute detail of their operation, but must trust that the small details are being addressed by their team. Micro—management will quickly become a curse on your organization and lead you in a downward spiral towards failure. Recognize micro—management, and act appropriately to avoid it.

Micro—management is often viewed as a test to determine if an engineer can successfully navigate the transition to the Manager

[41]

role. (i.e., a new Manager will be expected to leave engineering tasks to engineers avoiding micro—management)

The Encarta Dictionary definition for micro—manage: to control a person or a situation by paying extreme attention to small details.

There are times when micro—management is perfectly acceptable. These are when you are first demonstrating or instructing how a new task is to be completed and then possibly through the initial execution of the task by your staff. Staff members should be appreciative and not view this as negative management techniques.

The subject of 'Organization' has been covered at length in publications. Many well known authors have written about how to get organized. Review available books on time management and organization and make selections from reputable authors. There are some recommendations in an appendix at the end of this writing.

Organization should be viewed as a method to off—load the brain and not to burden it. Write it down and forget it—until it becomes necessary. You must develop a system (with tools) that gives you easy and quick access to what you need *when you need it.* These include electronic calendars, timed messages, SMS (Short Message Service), etc.

A clear desk and a blank white board are signs that a person is organized. Conversely, a cluttered desk and old scribbles on a whiteboard are signs that a person may be busy, but is not organized very well. Nobody is perfect so you should keep your work area midway between cluttered and ordered to the degree that works best for you.

Time is your most valuable asset, organizing effectively will optimize the use of your time. It will help to schedule everything, even time to return phone calls, review email or have coffee with an associate. I scheduled time every afternoon with Managers and sometimes an Administrative Assistant to go to the company cafeteria for a cup of coffee. Sometimes I did, and sometimes I skipped it, but it was always scheduled so that I'd always have time for it. It can be a valuable activity. We'd spend the coffee break talking about the day, about tomorrow, about people on the team that were performing exceptionally well, about the current business environment or what have you—but the atmosphere was always casual. If your work environment cannot accommodate this practice, be creative. Utilize whatever environment you can, such as a nearby coffee shop, to substitute.

Formal meetings should be preceded by appropriate preparation time. If a meeting or activity requires preparation work, then make an entry in your schedule for the preparation time—an obvious, but often overlooked, detail. How many meetings have you attended where you witnessed poor preparation by a key participant?

If you don't schedule it, it probably won't happen—or, if it does happen, then something important on the schedule will be dropped, forgotten, overlooked, or an opportunity missed. When you are organized, you become consistent and dependable—desirable attributes for leaders and managers.

[43]

Experiment with different methods and tools likely available in your organization. Many have found success with the to—do list. I prefer the electronic calendar because it is more effective for scheduling your day. Examples include those found in Lotus Notes, Exchange Outlook, Google Calendar, et al. Calendars provide for particular days and hours to be assigned to special activities. A quick glance can tell you what should be happening now and what's next. A to—do list only shows you what needs to be done and does not attempt to organize them within your limited schedule. You can integrate the calendar and to—do list, but be careful not to duplicate work for yourself by maintaining two systems. The electronic calendar has provided me with automatic event reminders, helping me to be consistent and reliable.

Time should be allotted at the end of every week or everyday to see what was completed, and what requires rescheduling. You must decide which incomplete tasks need to be rescheduled. As you attempt to reschedule activities, you must choose which activities will be dropped or rescheduled based on your availability, the availability of others, and the activity's significance to your goals. Place high—value activities such as implementation milestones or executive discussions at the highest priority. These activities are the ones that will produce the greatest benefit to you. Don't waste a lot of time on activities that produce little benefit.

Lastly, don't underestimate the value of scheduling your time away from work. Ideally, the entire weekend should be reserved for non—work activities, to unwind and de—stress. This will be particularly challenging for IT people managing 24/7 operations, but endeavor to arrange weekends in the way that you approach your daily schedules. However, weekends should be less structured, with a possible exception being a small block of time set aside for work. Events that should be on your weekend schedule may include your child's baseball game or recital or a jog through the park. If it is on your schedule, there should be no stressful surprises on Saturday morning.

Some choose to catch up on business messages on Saturday mornings. Some set aside an hour on Sunday evening to review the upcoming week's schedule or just catch up to be better prepared for Monday. Whatever you decide, try to make the weekend yours for you, your family and friends.

The technologies we have for organizing and setting reminders are abundant—use available tools and set a reminder for yourself—send an email; schedule an SMS via calendar; leave a voice message; etc.

Mobile devices can provide access to your schedule and access to emails almost anytime. Learn how to use one effectively. Organization or organizing activities (e.g., checking your schedule) may create stress. Learning to successfully handle stress is just another aspect of becoming a great leader. Another chapter is dedicated to the issue of stress on the job.

Be cautious not to become a prisoner of your chosen tools. Have you seen the father in the bleachers at Little League games typing on his Smart Phone? That is stress to be avoided. Give your full attention to the activity you are engaged in.

How you manage weekends at the office is particular to your business, but offloading weekend work tasks is a critical step towards giving yourself a break and reenergizing for top performance on Monday.

Proceed with the realization that you must repeatedly and reliably prove your abilities and your value to the organization. You are only as good as your last success, and more easily remembered for missteps. As a Manager of mine once told me, "One *Oh, shit!* wipes out a thousand '*atta—boy*s." This is true for most situations, but can be a bit of an exaggeration in some. An established reputation can help you through any "Oh shit!" as long as you are not consistently saying it. Plan carefully to avoid "Oh shit!" situations from occurring, but when it happens, utilize your good reputation and well earned respect to get through it.

Carefully consider each decision as you move through your day, assessing each activity's impact on your goals. Prioritize your time so that the largest percentage of time is spent on matters vital to your success—vital to achieving your goals. There will be other items that must be addressed—items that will necessarily steal away your time and not contribute to your goals. These include everyday items such as system maintenance, budget exercises, care for personnel, etc.

Classify daily tasks as *Vital*, *Necessary* or *Unnecessary*. Try not to give unnecessary items any of your precious time. For those necessary items that will consume your time, be as brief as possible completing them as best you can, delegating where possible.

The items you classify as being *Vital* to achieving your goals should be given the majority of your time and most serious effort.

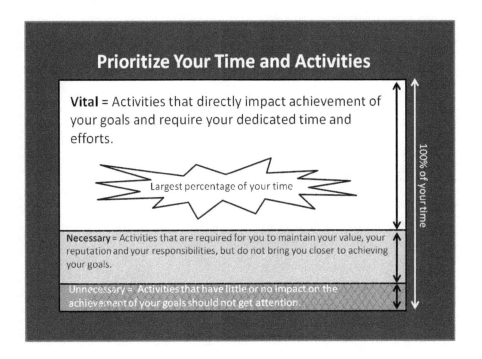

Illustration for time and activity prioritization

SYNOPSIS:

- Organize your work.
- Organize your team.
- Organize your information.
- Organize your time.
- Always be positive and respectful.

Organize your life! Be happy!

Chapter 4

Define Your Team

The term *team* is commonly viewed as a concept analogous to organized sports (baseball, basketball, hockey, etc.), but let's view it differently here.

Reflect upon all of the space missions you can remember reading about, watching on television (assuming you are old enough), or just talking about with your friends. The astronauts had to work as a team in order to accomplish the mission's goals. Truly, their very survival depended on the effective mechanics of the team. Each individual played a role and had various responsibilities that made that person a unique and indispensable member of the team.

Observe the 1995 movie *Apollo 13*. In that film, exceptional leadership is irreplaceable, and there are outstanding instances in which leadership is not differentiated by obvious methods (such as uniform or stars), and is fairly indistinguishable. The reason that it is indistinguishable is a tribute to mission leader Jim Lovell, portrayed by Tom Hanks. Of all the space missions you can recall, how many of them can you name the commander of the mission? The leaders in question remained almost anonymous by

[49]

successfully integrating themselves into the ranks of the team while maintaining their leadership role at a level that promoted camaraderie and took the spotlight off them to better promote the team. It is important that we are known for who we are—not by rank or title—but by our character.

There are several notable occasions where the character of Jim Lovell has to manage confrontations between Fred Haise (played by Bill Paxton) and Jack Swigert (played by Kevin Bacon). When tempers flare about the upcoming re—entry, Jim cools tempers down by properly putting things in their proper perspective interjecting: *Alright, there are a thousand things that have to happen in order. We are on number eight. You're talking about number six hundred and ninety—two.*

Jim Lovell demonstrates respect and appreciation during a silent period just prior to re—entry into the Earth's atmosphere, saying, *Gentlemen, it's been a privilege flying with you.*

The role of Flight Director at Mission Control, Gene Krantz, played by Ed Harris, has several outstanding examples of leadership, although a very different style as compared to Jim Lovell: Gene Krantz demonstrates **firmness** when he kicks a garbage can and demands results —*Goddamit! I don't want another estimate! I want the procedure! Now!* He demonstrates **compassion** when the astronauts tear off their bio—monitors and he asks the doctor, *Let's cut them a little slack, okay?* He demonstrates **humor** when he tells his support team that they must quickly come up with a procedure that can *make a square peg fit into a round hole*. Gene demonstrates positive **optimism** when the NASA Director, Gene's boss, tells him that *This could be the worst disaster NASA's ever faced*, and he replies, *With all due respect, sir, I believe this is gonna be our finest hour*. When the Mission Control team starts getting chaotic, Gene quickly **calms**, **unites**, and **motivates** them with one statement: *Let's work the problem people. Let's not make things worse by guessing.*

Leadership Characteristics demonstrated by Gene Krantz

Firmness
Compassion
Optimism
Motivates
Calm
Humor
Unites

There are dozens of fine examples of strong leadership that can be easily identified when the viewer is watching for them.

Notice also that the astronauts do not concern themselves with technical details previously addressed by the pre—flight teams, such as air mixtures in their suits or trajectory calculations. They trust in their NASA teams. *Jack, they've got half the Ph.D.s on the planet working on it*, is Jim Lovell's response to Jack Swigert's questioning of the NASA Mission Control team. This demonstrates confidence and trust in his team.

If your goal is to be a superhero and gain fame and fortune for yourself, then you cannot be a great Leader and will fail. That strategy may help you achieve great success for the short term, but eventually, you will falter. You will alienate followers, and they will slowly abandon you —first emotionally by not respecting your wishes, then physically by not completing the work to your standards—and you cannot work alone.

A Leader is best when people barely know he exists, when his work is done, his aim fulfilled, they will say: we did it ourselves.

—David Rockefeller

I am certain that neither Jim Lovell, nor Fred Haise, nor Jack Swigert would take complete credit for saving Apollo 13.

Consider your environment. Consider your situation. Above all, consider the people with whom you interact. The people you interact with are, by far, the

Integrate with your team.

most critical to success. Your team is a collection of individuals with individual lives, individual goals, and individual problems that, despite any similarity to yours, are very much their own. You must realize that as much as they like you, as much as they like the company, their first priority is themselves and their families.

Everyone on your team wants to feel important and needed, so determine who they are and how you can help them. You should ask yourself these questions regularly about everyone you have the opportunity to interact with on your team, always looking for opportunities to improve their lives. Offer solutions and assistance for their pains and frustrations.

List the individuals on your team and carefully define their roles. Then consider how the individual's roles impact the other individuals on the team.

Roles should complement the individual team members and should harmonize with the roles of others. You will see that some team members are more valuable to your success, but be warned, let there be no *prima donnas* (i.e., someone that thinks that they are very important or special, and whom is very difficult to please). They cultivate jealousies and distrust, either of which can destroy a team. The exercise is simple and quick. Do not underestimate its power as an aid in management.

Your IT Support Team	Roles & Responsibilities
Bill	
Fred	
Jill	
Joe	
Mark	
Sally	
Tom	

Simple staff chart with roles and responsibilities.

The size of your team will determine how much work this requires. If your team is large and Managers work for you, focus on the managers first. You should also know your Manager's teams, but not in as much detail as they should. It is helpful to at least know the names and positions of everyone within your organization. Be careful not to manage your Manager's teams, but demonstrate your leadership style to your Managers so that they clearly understand your expectations. Lead by example.

Where roles or responsibilities overlap or are duplicated, the leader's attention is required to maintain harmony in the team. The Leader must be the positive, motivating influence to minimize conflict.

Establishing a team—contact number, or group—contact line for which everyone on the team will be responsible, is strongly recommended. There will be many occasions where a single engineer will be working on a problem or project and not wish to be the callback contact, either because they will not be available or because it is a support team issue that matters to the entire team and must be answered. Assign an individual to collate messages, or create a rotating assignment for collecting messages left on the group line. Understand that this will be a line that no one will be anxious to answer unless you apply leadership to help your team understand its purpose along with your need and expectations from them regarding coverage.

The lesson is that you cannot lead an effective team unless you define and understand all roles and responsibilities before you try to bring about a harmonious dynamic. You must understand your environment in order to impact it in a reliably positive way. Start by doing something great for the team to boost morale.

An example:

While still fairly new to a Management position, I observed not only that my team lacked business cards, but also that they thought business cards important to have for vendor—team presentations. This was a simple, inexpensive item that could boost pride and morale, so I acquired business cards for each team member.

With the much—appreciated gesture of business cards for the entire team, I made sure not to differentiate titles, except for Supervisory staff. I learned early in my career, from working with a woman that purchased business cards with the credential Ph.D. after her name. Across the department, reactions were almost uniformly negative—it was as if she were plainly stating that she was better than everyone else. Not that she was wrong, but I decided there would be no such distinctions in titles throughout my team. A flat organization is best to promote superior camaraderie. If a person's talents or certifications exceed that of other team members, it will be apparent to most. You do not need a fancy title or acronym to show superiority. It will only cause bad feeling in the group. Even outsiders, such as vendors, will be able to recognize superior performers by their actions and by the respect they receive from other people around them.

Ask yourself what small actions you can take immediately to improve circumstances with your team.

Consider that your team is not an isolated entity, and that they absolutely must work well with other teams. This means that the goals of your team must be in alignment with the goals of other teams, within both the department and within the company. They certainly cannot be in opposition to the goals of other teams. When opposition of goals occurs between groups, it is up to the leaders to find a resolution and implement it as quickly as possible to avoid morale issues or operational disruptions. When meeting with your team, it will be helpful to discuss other teams, their activities, and how they might impact your team. Even though an organization contains many teams, in the final analysis, the company itself is just one big team, with a unified focus. Leadership skills must be applied at all levels to maintain this unity.

You want your team to be viewed well within the company. You want to—no, you absolutely must, be viewed as a team contributor.

Apply high levels of respect and positive actions towards other teams, peers, and your boss, but remain focused on your team. Team focus is essential for effective leadership. Your team is your responsibility and yours alone; if you manage it inadequately, the responsibility will be given to someone else.

I once found myself with a Manager on my team who was very disliked by his staff, whose peers showed him little respect, and who was not able to fulfill his responsibilities. I monitored for a time to give him a chance to adapt, but I had to remove him before he was there for a full year. His termination was a difficult period in my career. I behaved as professionally and considerately as possible, but it was clear—this person would now be out of work, and I would be resuming the Manager search. The guidance I received from my HR representative, regarding what to say and how to say it, was priceless.

We are all human, and all of us are prone to make mistakes from time to time. When you know you have made a mistake in your organization, it is best to quickly admit it, correct it, and move on—always remaining humble, positive, and optimistic, and never becoming defensive, pretentious or arrogant.

Chapter 5

Hiring Techniques

Hiring can be viewed as a painful task that must be done, or it can be viewed as an opportunity for positive change. You must view it as an opportunity for positive change.

In the most general sense, you are looking for a technically capable person that will be a productive contributing member of your team. You need someone who is intelligent and confident, but not arrogant, someone who can stay focused on the job at hand yet multitask effectively, and someone who works well in a team.

✓ technically capable
✓ intelligent and confident, but not arrogant
✓ can stay focused but can multitask
✓ works well in a team

Selection of a new employee is not difficult if you prepare appropriately. Create a list of attributes required for a position, and review the list with your boss. Your boss may have additional ideas or even opposing ideas. Listen and learn.

[59]

Scan through your internal and external networks for qualified individuals, or describe your needs to your network and ask for references.

Examples of desirable personal traits can include, but are not limited to:

- Energetic.
- Charismatic.
- Gracious.
- Confident.
- Cheerful.
- Optimistic.
- Possessing technical prowess.
- Well—presented and articulate.
- Team player that is not arrogant.

Create a similar list of technical requirements. Be specific, but not too detailed. Technical requirements should be appropriate for the level of position being filled (e.g.; Engineer, Supervisor, Manager, or Director). Do not discount a Manager candidate because technical certifications have expired. Current technical certifications are usually a negative attribute for a Manager as those people will tend to want to do everything themselves.

Prepare for interviewing: Once you have your list of attributes, separate technical requirements from personality requirements. Develop at least one specific question for each requirement on your list (i.e., at least one question for each bullet on your list, with a maximum of two questions per bullet).

Some examples of interview questions:

- Two to five technical questions specific to the area(s) to be covered.
- How would your previous boss describe you? Can I speak with them?
- How would previous teams describe you?
- How do you handle high—performance employees?
- Tell me about some of the things you have done for high performers.
- How do you handle underperforming employees?
- Have you ever had to terminate an employee? Please describe this experience. If not, describe how you would perform this action.
- What personality traits and practices do you value most?
- Tell me about a past success and how you handled it with your staff and with people outside your team. Did you promote it? How?
- Tell me about a past failure and how you handled it.
- What do you consider to be your biggest weakness, and what are you doing to improve?
- Why should I hire you?

Your list can be longer, but should not be shorter, based on your list of desirable attributes. I personally feel that popular questions such as; *Where do you see yourself in 5 years?* Or *Tell me about yourself.* are not very indicative of a person's qualifications. Answers to generalized questions like this will likely be rehearsed and will likely change once the person assumes their new role. Once your list is complete, review the questions to shorten the list even more, eliminating redundancies, making it very specific to your open position.

Your Human Resources (HR) representative should be aware of your needs and filtering applicants accordingly, so that you are not wasting your time interviewing people that are not qualified. You should provide HR with your basic requirements along with a generalized interview guide so they know what to look for.

Next, you need to establish your *two—mile test* for the interview process. The *two—mile test* is a method of screening applicants, and can be conducted within a simple phone conversation, saving both you and the applicant all of the time and preparation required for a face—to—face interview.

> *My son's high school soccer coach has a "two—mile" test that he employs to eliminate many of the students trying out for the school soccer team. On the first day of tryouts, the students are required to complete a two—mile run. Anyone who does not complete the two—mile run in less than 14 minutes is eliminated from team tryouts.*

Determine the criteria for your two—mile test. It can shorten and simplify your selection process. Your two—mile test can be technical in nature, (e.g., asking the applicant to describe the differences between CORBA and DCOM data base communication, or asking the difference between TCP and UDP protocol sessions). It can be non—technical in nature (e.g., ask the applicant to explain how they would go about establishing credibility quickly with the team or ask where they would concentrate their efforts in the first 90 days). Unsatisfactory answers should serve to eliminate them as a candidate for your open position.

A dialog is always best. Answers to the questions above are best achieved through dialog. Many people can give you the answers you are looking for to appear to be a winning applicant. For this reason, encourage dialog to learn more about the applicant's personality and communication techniques. Personal questions are not appropriate. However, a dialog will open up the conversation enabling you to more clearly understand the applicant's personality. Expect the applicants to ask questions related to the open position or about the organization. A lack of questions from the applicant should be a mark against them.

Ask a peer to take fifteen minutes to interview the applicant and regard their feedback carefully.

After you have interviewed the applicant, your decision to hire the candidate will be made on instinct. Observe the person's appearance and how they handle themselves. Determine if they demonstrate competence and confidence. If you don't feel good about your initial interaction with them, odds are they will not work very effectively with you. Your instincts will be most important; unfortunately, instincts are not very scientific in nature. You know your team and the teams of your peers. You know your environment. Consider your applicants working in your environment in order to speculate how they might perform.

Since your selection was not made alone, you can be confident that peers and HR will stand by your decision, good or bad. However, it is you that will be the primary recipient of the pride of a good choice or the pain of a poor choice.

Termination techniques require courage, nerve, tact, and experience. You should always be professional, and it is important to be as considerate as possible without being soft. Be confident that you are right in your actions regarding termination. Terminations have a very dramatic impact on the individual's life. Human Resources must be involved to protect you and the company. Your HR representative should be able to help. If not, ask them to find you help in the HR group. HR will engage the Security group if they feel it necessary. Your boss should be as supportive and helpful as possible.

Be strong, and do not proceed alone.

SYNOPSIS:

- List technical and non—technical attributes desired for the position
- Develop questions for each requirement
- Develop your two—mile test
- Work with your HR Representative
- Work with your boss and peers
- Make your selection based on the dialog and responses, but decide with your heart

Chapter 6

How to Bring a New Employee into Your Team

New employees sometimes pose an interesting challenge for integration with your existing team. Assuming you have done a good job with interviews and selection, the new employee will bring valued knowledge and new experiences, as well as a personality that will mix well with existing personalities on your team.

Be optimistically confident you know what they bring to the table and be grateful. A new job is a major milestone that has a tremendous impact on the individual's life. Be available for questions or casual discussions to help them to adapt and get comfortable. Think about what you need to do to get them engaged in the work and with the team as quickly as possible.

Suggested activities to engage a new team member:
- ✓ The new person's work area must be completely ready for work on their first day. Ensure it is equipped and supplied appropriately.

✓ Schedule an orientation meeting with the entire staff for the new employee's start (day #1 or #2). Inclusion is critical.

✓ Assist with online identification setup so that their online identity meets with your approval and will be embraced by the team.

✓ Order/specify appropriate business cards and stationary.

✓ Create a list of tasks for your new team member that will help orientate them and follow up for verbal reports on progress.

  * Engage them in casual settings such as lunches with you and the immediate team.

  * Is their area documented? If so, assign them the task of updating the existing documentation or, if it does not exist, have them build documentation. This is an excellent exercise for them to get familiar with the technical specifications of their area.

  * Monitor the setup of their work area to ensure it will fit within your standards. Your own standards should be in line with company standards and not overly strict (e.g., no explicit pictures, bad language, loud music).

  * Assign someone on the team to provide a tour of significant IT areas, introductions to personnel on other teams, and the company's employee facilities. The person you select should be a good match for the new employee's personality so you are not forcing too much too soon. Encourage note taking.

✓ Be available for questions or casual discussions to help them to get comfortable.

✓ If applicable, provide an introduction to the area's Administrative Assistant. Emphasize the critical nature of the AA's role in the organization.

✓ Provide introductions to Directors and the CIO as well as significant others pertinent to their job such as Legal Advisor and Financial Consultant.

✓ Business Leader introductions may be more appropriate after the first 90 days. Regarding the CEO, a meeting may not occur for years or they may never meet the CEO of the company, depending on company size.

For the first few weeks, attempt to maintain a daily dialog. As the new employee gets more comfortable, and as they become a valued member of the team, your direct interfacing with them will become less frequent. This is desirable. However, always maintain a regular (not necessarily daily) dialogue so that you never become estranged or unapproachable. A regular dialogue is professional and could be as simple as *Good morning!* or *How are you?* It can be that simple and require very little effort, but include their name in greetings to keep the relationship meaningful. Dialogue could also be in depth regarding their work or their family. You decide based on personalities. You will need to watch feedback, verbal or visual, as some people willingly invite different types of dialogue while others view personal questions as inappropriate prying. It can take months for you to ascertain the proper dialogue for each individual. Assumptions can be dangerous to relationships so be fairly certain and don't make assumptions. The less frequent your dialogue with an individual occurs, the more general you should keep the conversation (i.e., Determine the level of personal dialogue based on your level of familiarity with the individual.). The individual may invite further conversation if they are not intimidated and feel comfortable speaking with you, so be ready by listening for clues.

They are there for you and you are there for them. Treat them with the respect and gratitude due a valued team member.

To most effectively integrate your new employee, empathize and take steps to help them along in their transition. The new employee will benefit from your assistance immensely. You will benefit even more as an intelligent, new, comfortably integrated team member will be more valuable to you, facilitating more respect, more success, more acceptance, and thus giving you the best chances for future trust and empowerment from company executives. If your team looks good and does well, it reflects well upon you, the team Leader.

Do not take into consideration how you were treated when you first started, because it is of no importance now. Do the right thing for your new person.

There is an upcoming chapter dedicated to addressing how to 'Take Care of the People that Take Care of You' where this subject is discussed further.

Chapter 7

Educate — Leaders Learn, Adapt, Teach, and Inspire

All professionals have received some level of formal education. Education is a wonderful thing and will always help you. While some leaders fall back on their education to develop award—winning solutions, others have learned from experience and have also garnered great accomplishments. Don't depend on your education too much. An extended education is not a requirement for great leadership. In today's technologically fast paced world, your education can become outdated or no longer applicable to current technologies relatively quickly. When this occurs, to avoid obsolescence, you must work toward updating your knowledge through reading or certification. Your education must never stop. Typically, individuals with higher levels of education become pioneers or principals in their field. They tend to be *specialists* or *subject matter experts*—viewed by others as genius practitioners having great accomplishments to their credit that provided great advances. This level of accomplishment can never be over—stated. It is legendary when one of these brilliant individuals becomes a great Leader. Recent history holds many examples of great, specialized men leading without advanced educations.

For example: Ronald Reagan parlayed his mediocre college education (B.A. from Eureka College) with his moderate Hollywood fame and influence, into a great career in politics.*1 Reagan may not have been a genius, but he possessed strong ethics and surrounded himself with great people that he knew how to inspire and lead to accomplish great things.

Other examples include Henry Ford (who was a high—school dropout), and Bill Gates (who dropped out of Harvard). These men saw opportunities, learned how to take advantage of them, and adapted their lives to start businesses that enhanced their own lives and the lives of countless others, inadvertently inspiring millions worldwide. These actions required courage and commitment to a dream, as they were typically not encouraged by people close to them. Imagine the bravery that was required for a young Bill Gates to drop out of Harvard in order to start a risky enterprise in the budding industry of personal—computer software.

Conversely, many skilled leaders have advanced educations to their credit. As an example of the benefits that an advanced education can offer, consider Robert Metcalfe. An engineer, entrepreneur, and technology executive, benefitting from respectable educations from Harvard and MIT, Metcalfe specialized in networking solutions at Xerox PARC, inventing and developing Ethernet computer communications. He left Xerox, generalizing in business, to start up an early computer networking company in 1979 called 3Com.*2

[72]

Generally speaking, we learn (or are driven) to specialize in the early stages of our careers. Specialization requires specific education, which leads to unique experiences. Positive, successful experiences lead to respect among your peers. Think for a moment about how you specialized early in your career.

Education and specialization will provide a solid foundation for you as you progress into management and have opportunities to lead.

Arnold Schwarzenegger is great example of an individual that specialized (Body Building) to attain a leadership position (winning five Mr. Universe titles and seven Mr. Olympia titles), then leveraged that leadership position to expand his influence (business, motion—picture acting, politics) and follow his dreams. He was not an obvious candidate for any of these roles. His English was atrocious, and his meager education was barely adequate (a B.A. by correspondence from the University of Wisconsin–Superior), but he persisted. The rewards speak for themselves.*3

At some point, specialized education becomes counter—productive. When leaders stubbornly refuse to relinquish their specialization skills, they will be in danger of micro—managing their areas causing alienation of followers and eventual failure. As your career progresses, your ability to observe, learn, adapt, and inspire becomes more important than specialized education.

Arnold Schwarzenegger's specialization got him started. Generalization put him in the California Governor's chair for two terms, but I'm sure he has never stopped learning and never will. Great leaders are always listening and continuously learning.

Assess your team's individuals and discuss education opportunities. Team members can benefit from education in areas where there are gaps in knowledge. It can be technical or personal development that is important for the success of the team.

Like Arnold Schwarzenegger, great leaders never stop learning. There are education classes offered by Universities and Educational Consulting firms that teach you how to observe, learn, adapt and inspire. Utilize these resources to develop these skills in you.

They can help you move your career forward at a quicker pace and they warrant investigation. Books, such as recommendations provided in an appendix of this writing, also provide insight, but it is unwise to rely on one source. Many sources are available. Utilize self—help audio books to listen in the car or on your portable audio player while on the bus or train. Motivational speakers often make recordings and sell audio books. These are recommended when they are from respected, accomplished leaders with documented successes. See Appendix A.

*1 The White House—Presidents. Retrieved May 2, 2011 from
http://www.whitehouse.gov/about/presidents/ronaldreagan
*2. Robert Metcalf Biography. Retrieved May 2, 2011 from
http://www.biography.com/articles/Robert—Metcalfe—9542201
*3. Arnold Schwarzenegger Biography. Retrieved May 2, 2011 from
http://www.arnoldaloisschwarzenegger.com/biography.html

Select a trade magazine and subscribe online so that you receive a daily or weekly message that lists tests performed and topics discussed. These subscriptions are usually free of charge and provide much information.

Try each of these sources to determine which provides the most value for you. Often times, companies will not hesitate to pay for these education sources, but funding should not stop you because you are investing in yourself. You must have patience, since success does not happen overnight.

As a final lesson here—strive to "Inspire". Many people inspire and don't even know they are doing it. As valuable as inspiration is to motivating people, motivation has to come from within. Every team is unique. Determine how your team finds motivation and feed it with inspiration.

When you were young, remember how you got that school mate to run away when you challenged with "let's play tag"? The idea of playing, running, and having fun appealed to your schoolmate. You inspired that child to want to play with you. Inspiration really is that simple.

Think of a coach or teacher from your school days. They tried to inspire you to perform at the highest level possible, but the motivation came from within you. Some coaches were more successful than others. Think back: what inspired you to accomplish that challenging childhood experience? What were the benefits for all involved? Everybody must win.

When I was a child in Middle School, there was a coach, Mr. Carrigan, who encouraged me to go for the Presidential Physical Fitness Award. He helped me complete all tasks. When I had trouble completing the required sit—ups, he worked with me through several attempts until I achieved the award. His dedication and commitment to me have always stayed with me, inspired me, and shown me how to exude confidence, inspire, and motivate. He probably never knew how much of an impact he had on my life.

A good leader inspires people to have confidence in the leader, a great leader inspires people to have confidence in themselves.

—Eleanor Roosevelt

Many people know how to inspire, but for one reason or another, they consciously or subconsciously choose not to—*It's not my job!* To inspire people, you should find yourself sacrificing and liking it. The ability to inspire is a quality that is observed and learned. I have provided some examples of role models. Who are your role models? How do they inspire you? Observe them. Learn from their example.

I recently viewed a more contemporary example of team leadership on a newer television show. In that show, CEOs work within their teams and learn more about their team's daily activities and experiences in order to be a better leader. You too should become part of your team to learn how to inspire and motivate.

You must choose to adapt yourself to providing new ideas for inspiration. Be the individual Leader who regularly thinks outside the box, offering a different perspective to develop solutions that

[76]

benefit the entire organization. Role models are good for inspiration. Use them to inspire you to be better than the average Leader by way of innovation. Have the courage to be different. The rewards will outweigh any sacrifices required.

Never allow your title to limit your leadership abilities. Leaders are always watching for leadership traits in subordinates, so that they can help them along. Great leaders will help you in order to help themselves—surrounding themselves with talented people like you.

Show leadership talents to be given a leadership role.

Chapter 8

Take Care of the People that Take Care of You

Now that you have identified your team, who do you take care of, and how? Good Managers know that happy employees are loyal and productive employees.

Rule #1: Take care of your people so that they take care of you.

If your staff takes good care of their areas of responsibility, you will worry less and your bosses will be happy with your performance, requiring minimal attention.

First, identify which team member has a high impact on the team. What, ultimately, are your results? That person or persons can be a risk or can be your strongest asset (and can sometimes be both). If that person is unhappy and seems to dislike their position and function, your team will appear broken, and you need to work on one of the following two alternative approaches to fixing it. Both approaches will take time:

1. The first approach involves making the individual's world better where you have the power to do so. This means determining what makes them perform at high levels. What inspires them to commit? You must have patience while working with people.

When I started searching for the causes of my staff's unhappiness, the first thing I noticed was that there were two people on the staff that were generally recognized as more knowledgeable than the others and the team was not happy about it. Upon further investigation, I found that these two people were each known to be "the one to call" for problems and were getting paged at home almost nightly by our 24x7 Computer Operations staff (This was a time before cell phones became cheap and ubiquitous and technicians were still carrying pagers.). This nightly activity was a point of unhappiness for these two individuals and they wanted appropriate compensation.

A major change was required that would have an immediate and substantial impact. I ordered a "group pager". We established a rotating pager schedule and I worked with the Operations Manager to get the schedule to all his people and make sure they utilized it. The Operations Manager was very cooperative. If he was not, I was prepared to escalate to get done what I needed. After establishing a schedule, all my people took a turn with off—hours pager responsibilities. My two ace engineers were very happy about the reduction in their work loads and my other people were happy to help out and increase their contribution and value to the team. The action also increased the environment knowledge and value of the entire team.

2. The alternative approach is to mitigate the risk of a high impact person leaving (Don't underestimate its importance!). Prepare yourself and your team for that person's departure. You must establish a team member that can step up to the lost responsibilities should the person in question leave the organization. This requires role familiarization by another reliable, dependable performer and shared responsibilities. The significant individual, although seeing that you are improving their world, may not appreciate that someone else is learning his or her job role, especially if that person is also a high performer. This is often seen as a jolt to their 'job security' and a threat to their value. For this reason, you will need to maintain constant, daily communications with a sincere, upbeat, interesting dialogue in order to make that individual feel comfortable. They have to know, understand, and have their value to the organization (and to you) reinforced. Make it personal because it is a personal situation, and requires considerable attention. When explaining the critical nature of their role, how the company, organization and you benefit from, and require, their skillful, outstanding effort, they should understand why such a critical role requires a back up or contingency. Moreover, what would happen if they were ill and could not come to work? Most individuals would not want their own absence to jeopardize the success of the organization or company. Even though they hold themselves (and their family) at the highest priority, most do not want the organization to suffer because of their personal priorities. Most would rather leave on good terms. Also, they must understand the separation of personal and

financial goals. Although they are linked, they remain separate. Most importantly: be sincerely honest.

If this individual does not appear to be adjusting to this requirement for a back up individual and does not show an improved attitude (in a reasonable amount of time), you will want to make preparations for replacing that person as their exit is more likely.

If the criticality of the role requires immediate skills, you should consider temporary, external help, such as those offered by a professional consultant or contract technician. The consultant can learn the role and teach others in the organization how to perform it with or without the help of the departing person.

A consultant can also help motivate and encourage the person currently fulfilling the role by off—loading some less desirable tasks. When explained sincerely as an 'aid' to the position, a consultant will be a more acceptable option to this individual and this explanation can encourage mentoring. If the person is still resistant, it is a sign they are looking for work outside the organization.

Be sure to provide your requirements for the consultant in written deliverables. Keep in mind that this activity can cause discomfort with the person leaving and very likely hasten their exit. Be prepared by wording the consultant's contract so that the consultant will step up and fulfill requirements left by that person's exit. This can result in a contract extension, so budget appropriately. Do not fear becoming 'the bad guy'. You are only being honest and ensuring the success of the team and your own reputation. It is your job.

You may find yourself so impressed with the consultant that you offer them the vacated full time position, skipping the interview process.

When discussing the consultant's role with your team, remember to steer the discussion away from the classic negative stereo types that typically lead to alienation due to the temporary nature of most consultant contracts. The stereo types are easy to fall into and are mostly negative. Once the details are made known, the positive aspects of bringing in a consultant will outweigh the negative by far, or you wouldn't go this route. People will easily gravitate to the negatives, so make your intentions known. Stress those positive aspects that will benefit the individual(s) participating in the discussion. Make a sincere effort to integrate the consultant into your team, by sharing lunch, coffee breaks, promoting their activities with the team, etc. When your team and other teams see you embracing the consultant's contributions, they will embrace the consultant similarly.

Inspire to motivate your team. Reinforce the positive aspects of the job or the tasks at hand to inspire your team. Play down any negative points in favor of what can be gained.

Points of practice for an inspired, motivated state of mind:

[83]

1. A job that is enjoyed will be loved.
2. A job that is loved will receive the level of commitment required for success.
3. A job that yields success will realize financial rewards.

There are usually times when sternness is required, typically when the team gets into a dangerous situation. In those cases, when addressing an issue, try to never focus on people, but remain focused on the issue causing a problem. Conversely, when you are recognizing a job well done you should be focused on the person or people responsible. So for reprimands, focus on the issue or problem, and for recognizing performance, focus on the people.

— For reprimands, focus on the issue or problem, not the person
— For recognizing performance, focus on the person or people

Like the returns you expect for your sacrifices, team members will expect returns for their sacrifices. Plan for this. It does not have to be monetary. It can be as simple as a pat on the back, "IT Person of the Month" recognition, or more formal activities as allowed by company policy such as paid time off. However, remember that their sacrifice can be considered simply part of their job. Regardless, they will look to the Leader for explanation, for recognition and for reward. If the rewards are considered inadequate for the sacrifice, you will lose the commitment of your team.

[84]

Do unto others as you would have them do unto you.

—Jesus of Nazareth in the Book of Luke

What is most important to each individual on your team? Is it family, health, finances, career or all of these? Through daily dialog, you should gradually learn what motivates each individual. It is a simple formula and it is very effective. Once you find out what people's needs and desires are, start to address them to demonstrate that you care. When you care, you can help that person move towards setting goals and help them achieve their desires. For instance, if a sense of importance is what motivates them, let them know why you are expending so much energy to keep them, and reinforce their value to the organization.

Methods of demonstrating appreciation include:
- Sincere, daily, positive reinforcement through dialog
- Trade show attendance (expenses paid)
- Online education to immediately increase their value
- Technology certification to enhance their value and their career
- Other personal development functions such as a leadership class
- Additional responsibilities that will increase their contribution, value and confidence

Sincerely love your team. When it is not within your power to help them achieve everything they desire (e.g., a happy marriage, children, etc.), let them know that you sympathize and will do what you can to help. This can include time away from the job or business trips that include their spouses.

> *I once had to attend a 3—day meeting in Miami. My Manager allowed me to extend my stay through the weekend so that my wife could spend some time away with me. She flew into Miami on Friday night and we spent a fun winter weekend in sunny, warm south Florida. I was very appreciative, and my loyalty intensified. Are there opportunities like this in your organization?*

However, beware: you cannot allow time away for one of your team members when you cannot cover their responsibilities, and you will leave yourself vulnerable to disasters. You must be able to cover their area to protect the company from service outages. An alternate support person on your team can help facilitate this (*Teamwork!*). Responsibility for managing the area is your primary obligation to the company.

Do not proceed with any of these supportive actions while believing that the individual "will leave anyway". This is a negative belief, and may hasten their departure. You must maintain an optimistic outlook, believing that you can keep this person on your team. Treat personnel situations as if the employee will stay with the team forever (*risk*), but plan for their departure accordingly (*mitigation*).

Encourage socialization to help employees learn to work with others on the team. Socialization must be elective. You can provide an environment or event for socialization, but you cannot force people to socially interact with others when they don't want to. Encourage it, but don't force it. You can lead a horse to water, but you cannot make him drink.

Consider an office arrangement that encourages casual communication and interaction. Set up team workstations in close proximity to one another. Consider creating a technology lab for working together that includes a locking entry door.

Be prepared to consider methods for socialization that are not typically employed. Options include:

- Ball games
- Barbeques (at a park or at your house)
- Golf outings
- Fishing trips
- Charity functions

Vendors may offer you free tickets to gain your favor. You cannot allow this activity to influence your technology partnership decisions. Accepting tickets free from vendors may not be ethically wrong. You must decide, truthfully and ethically, for your circumstances. However, it is important to be cautious, as these activities may fall outside the bounds of company policies. If this is the case, then communicate both your circumstances and the anticipated results with your boss. He could sympathize with your plight and agree to share responsibility, or he could abide by company policy and forbid the activity. It will depend on your company. You will need to work within these constraints.

Do not work in secrecy where employees or company rules are concerned, because you will be jeopardizing your own career and those of your associates. If you feel strongly enough about the activity, speak to your manager's boss or approach your Human Resources (HR) representative. It is a good idea to work with them; they are there to help you. Always inform your boss of what you are doing, however, so that no one becomes frustrated by a perceived lack of transparency.

Remember that company policy is not the law, and that it can be adjusted by appropriate powers as needs dictate. The responsibility to convince your leadership, that the end result of adjusting policy will be the advancement or strengthening of the company's position, is your responsibility. Sell your goals. They must be ethical and respectable. If this activity intimidates you in your environment, seek alternative methods. Be creative.

Some recomendations include:
Create award programs that have the potential to make people feel good, such as "IT Person of the Month" or an "IT Gold Medal" award offered in a large, departmental meeting. These could have monetary rewards attached (e.g., dinner for two) that would be paid by the company. Gain permission to offer such rewards from your boss or HR representative. Even if rewards do not have monetary benefits, they are awards to be proud of, and will likely be within company guidelines. The simplest way to recognize superior performance is often adequate (e.g., simply tell the performer that they did a good job and that you really appreciate their efforts).

You will find that no matter what you do, or how creative you get, some individuals will never integrate with your team. They may be good people and have the potential to become good friends in the future. However, none of these characteristics alone will get them to where you need them to be. So in some cases, you will need to find ways to remove or terminate that person. It could be a positive action for all involved. It could be that another job function or another working location within the larger organization may benefit all involved. This would be an ideal circumstance. It is hard to do and difficult to find, so be prepared to search thoroughly. The environment and circumstances must be aligned to meet (or closely meet) expectations. There may be opportunities to align these, and you should search for them. Utilize your internal network first, because they have a vested interest in the outcome. Ask peers or ask your boss for help. In the worst cases, you will have to remove the person in the hope that they can find employment elsewhere.

Never lose site of the goal: to retain a happy, committed team member to fulfill a critical role in your organization—not to terminate. Your success will be measured by the degree of success you have taking care of the people who take care of you. Removal should be a last resort.

Demonstrate to people that you care and you appreciate.

Rule #2: Everybody has to serve somebody.

Get used to the idea that you are never finished and you can never do enough. Rule #1 has a tendency to take care of rule #2, but you should never forget rule #2. The leaders of a company, organization or functional unit will ultimately judge you as a success or failure so these are the people you will need to serve.

All leaders serve someone—even in the highest positions. Checks and balances are part of the democratic, capitalistic system in which we operate. Even the President of the United States, often referred to as the most powerful man in the world, must serve Congress, interest groups and the citizens of the United States. Frequently revisit whom you serve and remind yourself that it's all good.

Think about your unique situation. Whom does your boss serve? What are his goals? If you take care of your team and respectfully fulfill your responsibilities, your boss will likely be satisfied with your leadership.

Fortunately this rule works both ways. Regarding removal; after you have worked with your person, listened to their point of view, sincerely listened to their ideas, and feel there is nothing more that you can do to integrate this person to the team's ideas or your ideas; it is OK to be the boss and assert your authority. Even though you should hesitate to be the boss for these conversations, don't be afraid to assert your authority. At some point you may need to say that you understand their position, however, this is the way it must be. Ultimately, they need to serve you.

[90]

Note about Rule #2: Know it, understand it, and get used to it. That's life.

Professional relationships you develop can be beneficial to your career and the careers of your closest professional friends. When you change jobs and find that you need help, you should have a well developed network of professionals in the technology field that you can contact for help. Call on them if needed and hope that they will call on you when needed. Regularly reach out to maintain your network.

Chapter 9

Remember Why Your Team Exists

It is a common error for leaders to become so entrenched in what they are doing that they lose sight of their team's purpose.

For example:

A small team of highly skilled bakers was responsible for all baking activities at the bakery. The bakers were angry because they wanted to be true to the original French recipe for their cakes. However, customers liked the cakes with more whipped cream.

The bakers were confusing their mission. Their mission was not to bake the perfect cake, but to bake cakes that customers want to buy. Your mission, among others, is to make the necessary tools and ingredients available to your bakers so that they can bake the cakes your customers want.

Practice this lesson. You need to gently remind your team from time to time, why they exist—to provide a valuable service to the company. Not to provide the perfect service, but to provide a service that business people want to use. When business people like and use the service you provide, you magnify your value to the company.

> *My server support staff was complaining about the lack of scheduled downtime for maintenance purposes and wanted to take a server down without regard to stated business wishes. Agreeing that scheduled downtime was an issue, I politely explained to them their mission—their purpose: The servers needed to be available when the business declared they needed them. Ours was not to question why and when the business needed the service. The team was not happy about it, but they understood my point of view and agreed. They felt better when I explained to them that if the server crashed during business hours, I would explain to management that this outage could have been avoided, had we been given our requested maintenance window. At the time, we all knew that the chances of the server crashing were slim. Had there been a real threat, late night maintenance time would have been scheduled, despite complaints.*

As simple as this lesson is, it is often overlooked for more immediate needs such as security patch installations, memory upgrades or application fixes.

The needs of the business are most important, because without the business making money, the servers and their support team would not be required.

Measure all your efforts against the reasons you are here.

Just like with any service, the customer is always right.

Chapter 10

Document! Communicate! Communicate! Document!

Documentation and communication are skills that are often dismissed as trivial and unimportant. Build open and honest relationships using communication. Create transparency and build trust with documentation.

Set and manage expectations through communication. Do not operate in secrecy or try to execute without concurrence and support from the appropriate Managers.

Everyone is a salesman at one time or another. It is the leader's responsibility to ensure the values and benefits of any proposal are communicated effectively. Everyone is human and prone to make mistakes—you included. Since you know mistakes will come, plan for them by making allowances in time and budgets, and always own what you do—mistake or not. That means you should allow extra time in project plans and extra budget for the inevitable "gotchas". If they never occur, you should complete the project ahead of schedule and under budget (i.e., if there are "gotchas", you win, and if there are none, you win)

Once when I submitted an approved proposal for purchase, unbeknownst to me, the proposal was audited. The Finance Group representative sent my purchase request out for competitive bid and determined that the hardware could be acquired with an additional 1% discount. When I was called on it, I was able to produce a vendor quote with an identical discount. I explained that the numbers in the proposal were purposefully listed slightly high (1%) so that I could build in a cushion for the inevitable "gotchas". The Finance representative admired my intention, but disapproved of my method. He insisted I modify the proposal to reflect the best discount available and add a 'miscellaneous' line item to account for my "gotcha" concerns.

This example reinforces the lesson that integrity will help you stand behind anything you do. Do not be concerned about audits when you are operating with the best intentions and can show support (financial, technical, business) for any of your decisions. I did not anticipate this level of concern by the Finance Group, but I should have due to the amount of money being requested. If I had spoken with this Finance representative prior to presenting my proposal, we could have saved us both some time. Consider asking your Finance representative for advice prior to making your proposal.

Preach your mission, market your proposals and build procedures. Use whatever means you can to promote your proposal:

- casual "water cooler" discussions about goals and accomplishments (one or two — don't over—promote it)
- alert your boss when you have successes

- publically mention or award engineers or Project Managers in a departmental meeting
- Promote anticipated benefits in Change Meetings or Status Meetings and let everyone know about small successes

Be cautious not to over—promote or appear impetuous because people will start to avoid conversation with you. As a result of effectively promoting the project and emphasizing the values it will bring, team members will become passionate about the project. Business leaders will more eagerly cooperate by allowing the proposed change and encouraging business users. When financial leaders understand the benefits, they will more eagerly approve your budgets and support your endeavors.

Once you have successfully promoted the project, expectations will be high. You are personally responsible for meeting those expectations (i.e., doing everything in your power for successful implementation). Regular communication throughout the life of the project will help manage expectations. Representatives from the business (i.e.; stakeholders) must be engaged and be able to observe progress as the project develops. For this reason, having a business representative on the project team is recommended. If one is not provided by the business, request representation. Communicate all significant events with the business representative to keep them well informed of developments. Document all meetings.

Projects are excellent professional bonding events, but beware, almost everybody hates meetings—especially the weekly status meetings that have the same mundane agenda every week and have similar, albeit minimal results. Many are seen as a waste of valuable time.

When you avoid wasting people's time by communicating in other ways that more efficiently utilizes everybody's time, people will respect you for it and enjoy being on your project teams, which leads to higher levels of commitment and success. However, consider that face—to—face communication is sometimes best and usually irreplaceable. Circumstances usually dictate a particular combination of multiple types of communication. When you have a constituent that insists on weekly meetings, determine whether you can address their needs personally, as best you can, without holding weekly meetings attended by the entire project team. It may be acceptable to them for only you to meet with them weekly. Be "in charge" and make the right choices.

As an example: Several years ago, I was responsible for integrating departments from an acquisition. The business representative was a Finance person. He was extremely challenging to accommodate and was not particularly liked by project team members. He requested I hold weekly status meetings. I knew this approach would be detrimental to project team performance and serve to aggregate tensions so I needed to get creative and think of another way. I proposed to him that I phone him at the close of every business day to let him know what went on that day and determine if he had any issues that I needed to address. He was very happy with this arrangement and told me that he preferred it over the meetings he requested. I met casually during the day with significant project team members to obtain "on the ground" status. The daily phone calls to the financial business representative were made from my mobile phone, in the car while driving home, and were extremely productive. The team was grateful to me for handling it personally and not forcing them to attend weekly meetings. The Finance person was also grateful, and reported my creativeness, efficiency and willingness to sacrifice for the success of the project, to my leadership, advancing my status and respect among leaders and peers. My actions created a Win—Win scenario for everybody involved.

Face—to—face communication holds a value that sometimes cannot be replaced so do not underestimate its value. It is important for leaders to keep personal communications sharp. Consider face—to—face communication an opportunity for you to sharpen your skills and strengthen your professional relationships. When face—to—face communication is not utilized in favor of messaging or email, there is always the possibility for misinterpretation of your message or your intentions, so utilize face—to—face communications when you can. If you need documentation of any verbal commitments made, you must follow up the conversation with an email that reiterates your understanding of what was communicated verbally. A combination of methods is best. When face—to—face communication is not possible, consider conference calls over messaging to better project emotions such as gratitude and urgency.

Occasionally meetings are required. In those cases, schedule meetings consistently, but only when you have something to discuss that all parties will be interested in. Even though weekly status meetings are regularly viewed as standard for most projects, this should not be so. They are notorious for wasting time and may cost you some level of respect. However, they may be a requirement for major projects in your organization with multiple constituents. Based on your particular project, you must decide how often meetings are necessary and who should attend. Do not assume weekly status meetings are necessary or not necessary.

If weekly status meetings are absolutely necessary and it is not permissible to perform any alternative communications such as those shared above, ensure your meetings are as free flowing, brief and productive as they can be. Meetings that are overly structured with a rigid agenda will result in attendees loosing focus by thinking about other pressing issues (i.e., your project is likely one of several items consuming their thoughts). Conversely, if your meetings do not have enough structure they will likely become a waste of time and energy for all involved and not lead to progress or will not solve any issues. When leaders communicate project updates regularly, project team members gain confidence that they will be informed when there are any significant developments.

When you are hosting a meeting, a pre—meeting agenda is required to produce an effective meeting, so put an agenda together and have it in the meeting invitation. Do not distribute copies of the agenda at the meeting and do not rigidly follow it through the meeting. Utilize your agenda yourself to ensure you cover all the items that require attention, but do not cover it line by line. Keep your meetings interesting by skipping around your agenda as the meeting develops. Engage people in the meeting one—on—one, because most participants are eager to contribute and advance the project and will do so by speaking about their opinion or recent contributions. Several participants may have prepared something to present at the meeting so be open to reviewing what they produced. When you engage people by using their names it demonstrates your respect for that person and it acknowledges the importance of their contributions. By engaging each person in this way, you improve meeting involvement and keep the content interesting.

Follow up every status meeting with an email note summarizing the discussion and any agreements that were made. Be clear about commitments that were made and expectations for the coming days or weeks. Recipients of the note should include meeting attendees and Managers that have an interest in the project.

Communicate with business representatives as a matter of practice. Projects provide excellent opportunities to develop your relationships with business executives. Sincere, honest relationships will eventually bear fruit so foster relationships being friendly and sincere, never for personal gain.

Best practices for initial communication with business executives:
1. Identify who the key executive stakeholders are for the project. A stakeholder, as defined in Encarta's English Dictionary, is a person or group with a direct interest, involvement, or investment in something (e.g. the employees, stockholders, and customers of a business concern)
2. Obtain support from your IT Executive by enthusiastically communicating your intensions.

3. Call, email, or go see the business executive's administrative assistant to introduce yourself and request a 15 minute meeting with the executive.

4. Write down what you want to say and rehearse it. You are only asking for a few minutes of their valuable time, so don't waste it. Say only what you need to communicate: Briefly introduce yourself and your mission. Above all, communicate your intentions (i.e., why this meeting and their relationship with you can be very beneficial to them and to their business). Reserve preparation time for this meeting on your schedule.

5. Report the meeting results to your IT executive and include any agreements made with the business. For communication with the business executive, copy to your IT executive. Reserve time on your schedule to write the report.

6. Don't let the dialogue die there. Develop a relationship with the business executive with casual greetings; saying "good morning" or "hello" wherever you can casually run into them. Casual interaction and past meeting performance will help make follow up easier to obtain, so schedule short 15—minute meetings during the project just to update them with progress and benefits being realized so far. Eventually they will feel comfortable enough with you to forego the meetings for the sake of providing project status and will only wish to meet with you for major events such as a project delays, a cost over—run, a major milestone or accomplishment, or a significant change in plans.

Another communication that should be considered a vital component of project progress and must not be overlooked is with the IT Service Desk* (i.e., the Help Desk). The IT Service Desk must be aware of pending project milestones and must know the implementation well enough to be able to field calls from end users on the first day of production.

Examples of information sharing ideas include:

- Share significant project milestones and dates with the IT Service Desk Manager by utilizing email and face—to—face, verbal communication.
- Provide a half day tutorial in a conference room for people interested.
- Present a binder with technical documentation and Boolean procedures to the Service Desk Manager.
- Post a large map or a Boolean chart on an IT Service Desk wall
- Provide Week 1 technical support and escalation procedures to the Service Desk Manager or appropriate Service Desk representative

If the Service Desk looks bad, you will look bad, and your project will be perceived as a failure, costing you and your team the respect you have worked so hard to gain. You need to be certain the Service Desk is ready. Be creative and earn the respect you deserve.

It will be helpful to post a member of the implementation team at the Service Desk for the first day or week in production so they are available for agents to ask questions and obtain answers immediately. They don't have to take calls directly, but taking calls directly may be something you entertain on a temporary basis. It is more important that the Service Desk gains call experience while your team is present and available for questions. Typically, technical teams will object to taking calls directly. You will keep everyone happier by not forcing engineers to do something they object to, while still making their expertise available to Service Desk associates.

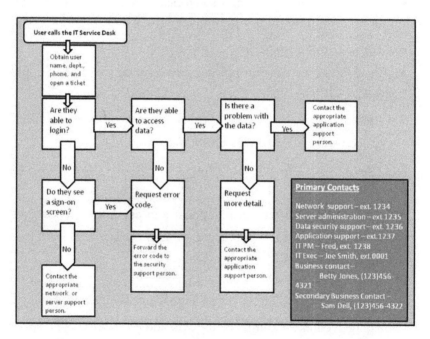

IT Service Desk sample Boolean Chart for an application deployment

The project cannot be considered successful until the business and Service Desk say that it is. Furthermore, the project is never completely over as long as someone in the business is using the service, so think of the service as long—term rather than something that will end on implementation day. Your responsibilities may change, but ITs responsibility to the business continues. If your wish is to separate your day—to—day contact with the project, first make sure you have done a good job with turnover to the IT Service Desk, because a poorly executed turnover will keep you involved with the project long after you recognize the need to move on.

Complete a successful turnover and you will develop a reputation of success, gaining a friend and ally with the IT Service Desk Manager. When you do your job well, you will develop mutual respect, friendship and alliances in the business that can help you in ways yet unseen.

Service outages offer another opportunity to communicate with business leaders. Do not wait for them to call you. Most leaders do not want to call you directly and will not be happy when they do, but they would love to receive a call from you. Give them a call and make them happy. Even if the news you bring is less than satisfactory, they will be happy to hear from you—to know about what is happening in their environment and that you care.

Lastly, the value of detailed and accurate documentation cannot be overstated. I have seen too many accounts where documentation was either non—existent or outdated and inaccurate. It is nearly impossible to effect positive change upon any technical environment that is unknown to you. To find and exploit opportunities, you must know your environment well. The way to know your technical environment well is through detailed, accurate and current documentation.

Take the needle in the haystack for example: Imagine being tasked with finding that needle when you knew absolutely nothing about the hay stack, other than it is big – very big. Now imagine if you knew every straw of hay, its location, its thickness, and how it interfaces to other straws of hay. As a real—world IT example: Your Wide Area Network (WAN) can be a hay stack if you allow it to become so.

Glance at the following diagram and decide which version of this WAN document you would rather have at your disposal for making tactical or strategic decisions.

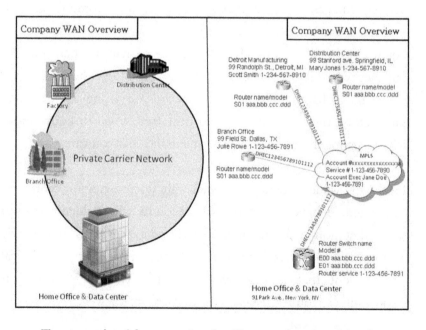

Two examples of documentation that illustrate the value of detail

Always be vigilant to keep information accurate. A final step in any change procedure must be to update documentation.

Individual location detail should be added to aid in design change planning and trouble—shooting such as the following illustration. It will be helpful for budgeting future contracts, planning upgrades, etc.

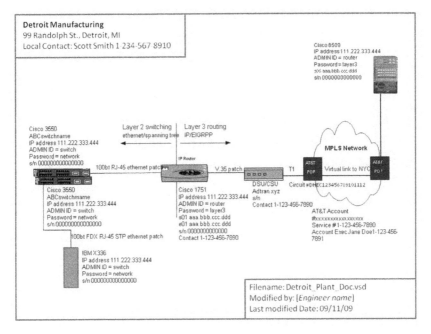

Remote location detail example

Remember to keep your boss informed of significant events in their environment, whether it is in regard to a project for which you are responsible, an outage, or any other notable event in your area. Utilize documentation to illustrate your situation and to help

[107]

your boss understand the risks. Do not overlook your boss or your boss's concerns. If you neglect your boss, you will fall out of favor, and will risk being replaced.

Documents can be created with off—the—shelf products that you probably already have. Create document names with uniform and simple text that are easy to understand (e.g.; Detroit_Plant_Doc.vsd). The documentation is of little benefit to you or your organization if the information is cryptic, sloppy, or hard to find, and cannot be utilized easily by others. There is no need to buy specialized tools for this purpose. Microsoft Windows Office Suite, HTML, or other readily available technology and hardware can be utilized. Create an information data base utilizing tools you already have. Be proud of what you build. Evangelize the benefits and importance of good documentation among your team and encourage others to use it. Provide access to the database to your team. Provide read only access to people outside your team.

------

* ITIL

The Information Technology Infrastructure Library was developed in 1988 by the UK government, to provide guidelines and specifications for IT services operations and management. ITIL is the most widely adopted approach for IT Service Management in the world. It provides a framework for identifying, planning, delivering and supporting IT services to the business.
Definition retrieved May, 2011 from
http://www.itil—officialsite.com/AboutITIL/WhatisITIL.aspx

* IT Service Desk

The IT Service Desk (a.k.a. Help Desk) is a component of the Information Technology Infrastructure Library and is the single point of contact between the service providers and the users. A typical Service Desk manages incidents and service requests, and also handles communication with users.
Definition retrieved May, 2011 from
http://www.best—management—practice.com/gempdf/ITIL_Glossary_V3_1_24.pdf

Use documentation to identify opportunities and communicate.

[109]

Chapter 11

Build Operational Procedures

To determine where operational procedures can make a substantial improvement in your area of responsibility, ask yourself the following questions, listing possible answers and actions you can take.

- How does your organization operate?
- Do technical changes occur randomly or are they coordinated between different teams?
- What are the active projects in IT and when are they scheduled for turnover to the IT Service Desk and production teams. How can they become better known?
- Will there be conflicts? If you don't know, find out. If you think you know, confirm it.
- Where is there disorder or chaos that can benefit from formalized procedures to help your organization be more efficient and more successful?
- How does your team interact with other IT teams?
- How does your team interact with the business?
- Is existing technical documentation adequate for all systems or do some systems remain a mystery?

- Who is assigned responsibility for what? Organize your organization!

If the answer to any of these questions is unclear, the Leader must determine a method to acquire the information. If a process is not documented and shared, it does not exist. No matter how simple it appears, it must be documented and shared—even enthusiastically evangelized. The organization leadership needs to inspire their teams to create and support formal IT processes.

A good mix of structured and entrepreneurial culture is best. We need the entrepreneurial thought process to move forward creatively and make improvements, but we need structure so that things do not get out of control. Positive, creative change is a great example of entrepreneurial spirit while the Change Management Process is a great example of structure.

The importance of Change Management cannot be overstated. It ensures no changes are implemented without the knowledge of all those affected. Many software packages are available that include a change request form that is submitted online for review by IT teams. However, a special software package is not required for managing change. Managing change is one of many processes utilized by a successful technology team. The ITIL provides lessons and examples for each process. To familiarize yourself with basic but essential elements of an IT Change Request form, review the sample shown below:

Online Change Request Form	Unique Change Number: 123ABC
	Date Request submitted: 10/20/11

Location and description of requested technology change:

Date requested: [_____]   Time requested: [_____]

Business Case and description of risk to the user community:

Description of Testing for a successful change: Description of back-out plan:

Success criteria:

Manager responsible for change: [_____] Phone [_____]

Responsible backup contact name: [_____] Phone [_____]   PRINT

Authorizations: [_____]

Signature: _____

Signature: _____

Sample Online Change Request Form

For a more detailed description of ITIL Change Management
see http://www.itilchangemanagement.net/.

In any managed environment, especially IT, controlling change is
absolutely necessary to provide a reliable, high performance service
to the business.

Submitted Change Request forms should be reviewed by
representatives from all IT teams in a meeting where changes can
be discussed until they are understood. The meeting coordinator
should produce meeting notes that document all discussions for

[113]

future reference and for review by non—attendees such as high level Managers or Operations staff.

Change Request Process Meeting Notes	Meeting Date: _____ Page ___ of ___
Meeting Coordinator: _____	
Attendees: _____	
Change number: _____	
Date and time of change: _____	
Change approval: _____	
Special Considerations:	
Manager responsible for change: _____ Phone: _____	
Change number: _____	
Date and time of change: _____	
Change approval: _____	
Special Considerations:	
Manager responsible for change: _____ Phone: _____	

Sample Change Request Meeting Notes

Documented processes shared properly are hallmarks of a well run IT environment. Procedures benefit from a detailed document that is shared with your team and possibly other teams. Not every team member will like all procedures, but it is up to the Leader to confirm everyone understands that this is the way things must occur and why. Provide positive explanations that reflect the greater good.

Technical documentation is invaluable for trouble investigation and for tracing what was done during implementation or changes.

[114]

Technical documents specific to your environment are similar to vendor documents for technology products, but the documents are unique and specific to your environment, reflecting your particular implementation of this technology as utilized by your business in your environment.

Documentation can be textual or graphical, but should be a combination of both to aid the reader through interpretation, because although you can assume, you can never predict who the document reader will be. Therefore, build the document so anyone can read it and understand it. Ensure documentation updates occur when changes are implemented. Periodically confirm documentation accuracy.

*Sample of unique, environment specific, technical documentation
(Detail includes device types, module types, specific slot installed, technical
contact, file name and date of document)*

For information accuracy and sharing, most companies require their Managers to create formal job descriptions. They clarify each person's role in a document that is shared with and understood by HR. Purposes for job descriptions include, but are not limited to:

- Provide a standard structure and instill a discipline for employees to understand and build job function documentation that is clearly understood by all. Misinterpretation of roles and responsibilities will be prevented.

- Provides a clear description of the role for HR when searching for new candidates
- Clarifies employer expectations for a new employee
- Provides the basis of measuring your employee's job performance or for discipline issues.

Formal processes, procedures and documentation have a place for building success. Assemble, formalize, share, and live them to gain respect, order and happiness. In this cause, you should expect sacrifice from team members so communicate your expectations, but no sacrifice will be greater than the Leader's.

[Company Name] Job Description

Title: Information Technology Engineer
Reports to: Manager of Technology Services
Work location: Address, City, State

Job responsibilities:
To plan, implement and support technology solutions as deemed appropriate, to maintain reliable, high performance systems in accordance with agreed management plans.

Key responsibilities and accountabilities:
* Maintain and develop systems ......
* Plan and implement new systems as ......
* Develop ideas and solutions for ....
* Participate in support team activities as specified by......
* Work hours as required by job responsibilities stated.....
* Report on activities and.....
* Maintain and report on equipment and software performance for.....
* Attend education to develop skills as required by.....

Technical Skills Required for position:
* Unix Administration
* Understanding of Relational Data Base structure and performance
* Detailed knowledge of TCP/IP communication

Qualifications:
* Minimum years experience performing .....
* Must be familiar with technology system.....
* Ability to read and write in a technical format.....
* Presentation skills.....
* Tools of the job.....

Candidate must be willing to perform all job requirements as required.

Sample Job Description

Chapter 12

Nurturing Ideas, Creativity & Innovation

In any Information Technology environment, you will come across challenges that require innovative solutions. The solutions cannot be conceived without intelligent people who understand the technology and understand the problems clearly.

A problem or efficiency issue will sometimes present itself to you by chance. Great leaders will not wait, but will seek them out. Continuously review your environment and foster the spirit and desire in your team to regularly review their environment and circumstances. Encourage action today to avoid more undesirable actions in the future (e.g.; share the discovery, share ideas for a solution, act soon or react later). Your team will agree that doing things right the first time will spare them great pain later.

When a challenge is brought to light, learn as much as you can about it. Utilize the knowledge of your technical staff and resources available in the line of business. Bring your team together to review the challenge and develop a solution and implementation plan.

You will probably have a solution in your mind and a plan to implement it. Bring your team together just as if you do not have a solution and observe what ideas the team introduces. After you have heard your team's ideas, suggest your ideas and request feedback. A good team will develop similar or better ideas in the meeting. Your original ideas will likely change after input from your team is considered. It is best if your team feels that the solution is a joint development—*We did it!* Remember: Don't be a hero. Claiming the idea as your own may be good for your own ego, but it could stifle the idea process in your team, and your goal should be to nurture the solution—idea process, not to stifle it.

For example*:*

> *Several years ago, at lunch, speaking about the monthly phone bills received that morning; I observed the Far East regional offices were producing extremely large bills calling internationally between offices. A top engineer on my team offered to investigate the calling practices to learn why the costs were so high. Pleased to be getting help without asking, I encouraged him, with enthusiastic approval, to get started right away. After a short investigation, he determined that inter—office fax was generating frequent, long calls between countries. The team was brought together, and we decided to obtain pricing for a private network and fax over IP gateways. The private network was implemented, fax gateways were purchased, and three of the offices received voice over IP gateways, reducing annual operating expenses by more than a quarter of a million dollars annually. The individual, who originally volunteered to investigate, was encouraged to present our solution to executives. Funding was approved, and the project was completed successfully. Engineers were exposed to leading—edge technologies like FoIP and VoIP (Fax— and Voice—over IP).*

This type of investigation and solution development can be applied to any IT situation in which costs are noticeably high. Find out why costs are high, and bring the engineering team together to analyze the opportunity and develop a creative solution to reduce costs.

The success was viewed as a team success, bolstering camaraderie and respect for the team. Incidentally, respect was garnered for the Team Manager as well. This illustrates the difference between a good team and a great team—after all, a good team could have left the status quo, and the company would be spending a quarter—million dollars more to operate in the region, and, no one would be the wiser. My team was exceptionally happy with themselves – not only for this accomplishment, but for the innovative ideas and leading edge technology they introduced. The Far—East regional offices were very happy with the systems we put in. They subsequently increased inter—office communication, resulting in further (unanticipated) operational enhancements and efficiencies. The technology utilized is not as important as the efficiencies that were gained and the money that was saved, or the initiative demonstrated by great IT support teams—both at HQ and in the Far— East regional offices. Happy people tend to work together better and produce more.

After ideas are accepted and the implementation process has started, there are still opportunities for innovation. Encourage your team to innovate, but be careful not to encourage martyrdom. Martyrs take unnecessary risks for their own recognition. Encourage team members to share ideas with you and with the team. Martyrs will quickly become alienated from the rest of the team, and become detrimental to success because of their need for personal recognition and notoriety.

The definition of Martyr from Encarta English Dictionary: somebody who makes sacrifices or suffers greatly in order to advance a cause or principle.

In cases where team members play the hero and make unplanned adjustments, they must be directed to correct this behavior. This behavior can be counterproductive not only for team morale, but also for the quality of service that your team provides for the business. I call these people "cowboys". You cannot be a successful Leader with cowboys on your staff. To inspire innovation and sharing, be creative in explaining that each individual plays an important role in the success of the team and organization, and that their actions are very important to you and the team, but that any new ideas or suggestions must be shared and discussed with the team.

If the individual's behavior cannot be corrected, then the individual must be removed from the team. You also need to be creative with removal.

An example of creative removal:
I observed an individual correcting an issue on his own, midday, without first consulting me or the team. It was admirable initiative, but I needed to explain to him why this activity was unacceptable. He agreed, and said he would not do it again. The second time I caught him doing it, I explained

that I cannot tolerate this behavior on the team. He agreed and once again, said he would not take the risk again.

Weeks went by without incident, although I suspected his actions continued, because I did not feel his statements were sincere. Eventually, his activities came to the attention of Executives and, as the Manager, I was held accountable. Now, my Director was forced to get involved. His input was invaluable to me. He was tactful and innovative. Our reputation was at stake, and he assumed the responsibility of preserving it. I admired his actions, and was grateful for the help.

I needed to remove the offending individual, so we discussed his aspirations, and jointly decided that he would be better placed on a graphic—design team that was a bit more free—spirited and did not have rigid guidelines for daily operations. My initial feeling was to punish this person, but our long—term feelings for this individual were ones of respect, and we really had no desire to make things bad for him.

This move was a win—win scenario since he was able to do something he liked, and the graphic— design team was happy to have him. I was able to hire a new person to serve in the newly vacated position, and the new person was just as skilled, fit into the team well, and made the team more complete. It became an opportunity for fresh ideas and improvements (i.e., Win—Win).

Whatever technological innovation you can develop in your organization, TCO (Total Cost of Ownership) and ROI (Return on Investment) trump all. You may have great ideas or develop outstanding innovations, but if the TCO outweighs the investment and the ROI stretches beyond a sensible duration, you should let it go, to be revisited at a later time, after circumstances and the technology have matured.

TCO is not always apparent as the situation in the business environment can change during the implementation and costs can change. The best you can do after realizing a disappointing TCO is to understand what happened, salvage from damages, strive to prevent similar situations in the future and seek acceptable adjustments or alternative methods. Do not let disappointment discourage future ideas and innovation. Never try to hide a failure. Admit it and own it, confident that your motives were the best.

For those ideas that don't work out well, always chalk it up to a good experience. Some refer to these as "good failures", or ideas that, for some reason beyond your control, did not work out as planned. Criticism should be avoided and instead, focus your review on the why and how to move forward from here.

If you don't make mistakes, you aren't really trying.

— Coleman Hawking

Talents I found to be most important for innovation:

Vision — the capacity to have an open mind, to see the way things are, and the ways things could be
Creativity — the genius to apply technological advances in innovative ways to the advantage of business practices
Analytics — critical analysis of situations and ideas

Enthusiasm — passionate interest in or eagerness to engage

Courage – the ability to take risks and follow your thoughts and feelings with action

Emotional Leadership — the ability to encourage trust, inspire creativity, engage passionately, share the vision, and inspire others to dream more, learn more, do more and become more

Chapter 13

Embracing Change

Change is sometimes an elusive thing to identify, but it is ever present. Change can be good, if you embrace it for the opportunities it can present.

For example:

The Atlanta sales office expressed a desire to enter orders any time during the day. Currently they were waiting until the end of the day, connecting and entering all the day's orders. This was not only inefficient, but inconvenient and expensive for them. Thinking that the other North American regional sales offices might have similar challenges, I contacted them. They did. Now here was an opportunity to make communications more efficient while at the same time, empowering the sales offices to increase sales, enhancing company revenue opportunities. A private network was implemented for three regional sales offices and all expectations were realized. The activity allowed me to gain respect with both IT management and with the business. Each activity builds on the previous one and everybody wins.

If you do not embrace opportunity, you will find yourself reacting in an undesirable way. This example of business changes (Sales) could be addressed with technology changes (Access Networking). You probably have business processes already in place that could be enhanced by new technology developments. Mobility technologies and unified communications provide excellent examples where we can enhance or improve business performance through the introduction of new, enabling technologies. These technological developments, when added to your business, can enhance your value (and your boss's value) to the organization. Seek ideas from your team. Seek out allies in the business communities.

Architecture development activity:
1. Produce a list of a few business functions that you are aware of.
2. Create a separate, unrelated list of new, enabling technologies.
3. Bring your team together to discuss the two lists and develop ideas, attempting to match technology solutions to business functions. Be prepared and receptive for the team to add additional business activities or new technologies. You are embracing change and encouraging your team to embrace change by leading them to realize the opportunities that change can create.
4. Discuss how a selected technology can help the business so that the team clearly understands their mission and potential value to the business.

Maintain a dialogue with your allies in the business community. You can keep the conversations casual, but attempt to determine what they are doing and inquire as to what they have heard about technology—what technology they are talking about. This type of casual dialogue keeps you in their mind and allows you to keep abreast of what is important to the business. You are watching for change. You become the team player on the business team providing the power of technology—one of the gears in the money machine.

Whether your customer is internal or external, your IT role must be that of a sales person, so strive not to be a "no" person, but a person more likely to be open to new ideas and discussion. Portray yourself as a "can–do" person, because when IT says "no", IT is typically viewed by the business as an impediment to achieving goals. Rather than saying "no", be receptive and sincerely interested by replying "possibly" and ask to talk about the request in more detail; to dig deeper into where the request is coming from and why it is deemed necessary. Be positive. Request some time to review the requirements with your team. Offer alternatives or modified solutions; services you can effectively provide and support, elaborating the business advantages. There is always a danger the customer will go elsewhere for the services they desire, bypassing your services and creating more problems for your support team later on. Any good sales person will tell you that saying "no" to a customer request is a sure death sentence. Conversely, becoming a "yes" person is dangerous as it will become more difficult to reply to requests with "possibly", and

> *Don't be a "no" person, but a person open to new ideas and discussion. Be a "can-do" person.*

being known as a "yes" person can be incredibly stressful as a "Yes" resolve may be extremely difficult to support and lead to failure. Constructive dialog is always best.

Utilize vendors for their knowledge of their products or services in your environment and their experiences with other customers. Vendors can be a great value to your team by bringing skilled engineers to bear on technology issues you are facing. Vendor services can be made available to you at no cost, if you skillfully build your relationship with them. Vendors are in your company to sell products or services. If you are purchasing these from them, don't hesitate to ask them for complementary help should you need it. If you do not ask, they will likely not be offered, so ask. If you ask and they will not assist you, you might want to consider a new provider. Once again, you are looking to achieve a win—win situation. Treat the vendor's engineers like part of your team. Communicate to your team that the relationship is a partnership, and while working on problems, they should learn as much as they can from the vendor's engineers. They will have much to teach about their products or services. The vendor engineer will learn how their product is utilized in the real world. When treated properly, with respect and consideration, the vendor's sales representatives and engineers will enjoy visits to your company—or at least prefer visits to your company over their other customers. This is precisely the relationship you should foster. Imagine having a handful of highly skilled engineers at your disposal for no cost. There will be times when the vendor's engineer you want will not be available when you ask for them, but with a large resource pool, the vendor will be able to engage another engineer not as familiar with the account, but extremely product knowledgeable. The vendor's talent pool is likely much deeper than yours. Be grateful for their willingness to assist you.

Vendors should be considered partners when their role in the partnership is:

- Learning your environment and how their product fits.
- Learning your responsibilities.
- Learning your pains and offering you solutions to reduce them.

A vendor that meets with you for the first time and attempts to make a sale is not a vendor that you should welcome back into your company—ever.

If, in the first visit, the vendor attempts to learn about your situation without selling, then you should consider them a potential partner. If they can help you be more successful by learning your environment, presenting you with solutions, and working faithfully with you to ensure that a solution works in your environment, you have found a great partner and the vendor has earned a new, loyal customer.

The vendor must have an established working relationship with you long before you issue the big RFP. The initial contact should not be an RFP response.

It may be possible for your company to partner with the vendor on a shared charitable interest (e.g., charity events, or promotions).

The larger technology vendors will be active in charity work, and will see value in partnering with their customers. Once the charity relationship is initiated by you, your involvement should be minimal. Many companies, including yours, may have individuals or entire departments dedicated solely to this activity. Ask your Human Resources representative. This activity strengthens the relationship between your company and the vendor so it is up to you to have the courage to be a Leader and kick start the process.

The only constant is change, continuing change, inevitable change that is the dominant factor in society today. No sensible decision can be made any longer without taking into account not only the world as it is, but the world as it will be.

— Isaac Asimov

Do not be afraid to take a risk when it is called for. Any risks should be calculated carefully and you must have a plan to mitigate any risks (i.e., a backup plan or safety net). Taking risks to create improvements is what great Leaders do. Success is never guaranteed, it is the Leader who must ensure success. When failures occur, and they will, it is the Leader who must embrace the failure and determine how to turn the failure into a positive situation where opportunity can be found and creativity fostered. You will likely never be criticized for trying to improve a situation. Have a plan, and you can effectively mitigate risk and build success.

Chapter 14

Promote Your Team and Advertise Accomplishments

It is the Leader's responsibility to let everyone know how good your team is and how much they contribute to the organization. You work hard to build a first class team. Ensure people know about it. There is a right time to boast.

For example, during a major hurricane and flooding, a local TelCo switching station became flooded. Most companies in the area were forced to shut down or delay global operations.

Because back up communication services were planned, tested, available and utilized, our business was barely affected. My team, realizing this was a real and serious disaster, worked long hours and made themselves available at any time of day. This did not go unnoticed by the business divisions affected. They knew the other companies in the area and how good they were supported by my team. However, it was more or less expected by IT management and very little attention was paid. As the Leader, I needed to let the IT leaders know that extra preparation and commitment was given here to provide a premium service with high availability to the business. Without this preparation, effort and dedication, the national and global businesses would have lost revenue.

[133]

It was a matter of principle that my staff be recognized, so I created a short note to my boss, explaining how my staff went above and beyond the call of duty. We received only recognition and a pat on the back, but that was satisfactory. Positive recognition equals respect.

Sacrificing team members were given paid time off. In addition, I provided engraved, pewter mugs to everybody on the team. The mugs were ordered online with an engraving that referenced the event and were expensed to the company. For such a small cost, I was able to express my appreciation for the entire team. It was greatly appreciated by the engineers, boosting pride and team morale, as demonstrated by mugs being proudly displayed for months after the event.

As the Leader, you should always be looking for small opportunities such as this, to show appreciation for your team.

Leaders need to be creative to show off the skills and commitment of the team without being repetitive or ridiculous. Remember that you are expected to do well, but for those occasional circumstances where performance is exemplarily, a little boasting is justified and appropriate.

A wonderful way to show off your team's accomplishments is to put it on a poster and place the poster in a strategic position. It can be an online banner or a printed diagram. Examples include:

- The home page of a ticketing system.
- A large printed network infrastructure map, in poster size, placed in a hallway or on the wall outside the CIO's office

- A map of the virtual cloud similarly placed.
- A map as Windows wallpaper.

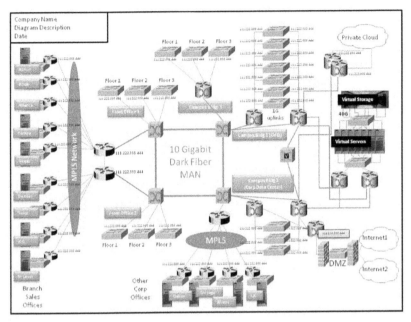

Poster of a Global, Corporate Technology Map

Promoting, marketing and advertising are important components of great leadership, whether it is people, technology or business, and can serve to advance your mission.

Promote your team and your contributions.

Chapter 15

...and Then There's Your Boss

There is a simple strategy to follow regarding your boss. I will use the pastry analogy again:

> *Think of IT as baking a cake: If you add all the right ingredients in just the right amount, and bake it at the correct temperature for a precise amount of time, you end up with a great cake.*

I'm sure you can see that there are no great secrets to making a great cake, yet not everyone believes they can do it. Great leadership and superior management are not great secrets either, and anyone can do it with the proper commitment, sacrifice and good people.

Just as with a great cake, you need to use the right ingredients of people, procedures and technology, mixed just right and properly coordinated over a set time at a specific intensity, to come out with great results. Everyone will inject their own personality to execute this work in their own way. Common tools are humor and structure. Be approachable. Do not allow yourself to appear foreboding or threatening. Needs don't always fall between nine and five so be prepared to spend extra time when necessary.

Prioritize your leadership efforts:

1. You work for your team.
This is the sacrifice for your team that is mentioned repeatedly.

2. You work for your boss.
Loyalty surfaces here. Your boss is your first line of acceptance and rewards, so treat your boss with respect and dignity. Do your job well, and your boss will be happy with you.

3. You work for your organization.
Your value to the company business shows here. This is in large part perception. If your contributions are not obvious, make them known. You will improve perception and increase your value to the company.

4. You work for your profession and your own personal development.
There is nothing wrong with taking care of yourself and your future, as long as you serve the needs of the business. If you do not take care of yourself, you will lose respect and inhibit your potential. Many will argue that this should be your highest priority, but I disagree, because in addressing the higher priorities honestly, passionately and completely, this last item will become an incidental product of the higher priorities and will not require extra time and attention.

Do not exclude your HR representative because they may be able to help. The Human Resources group is there to help you succeed.

They can help in unexpected ways, so always consider them before making personnel decisions or company impacting decisions. I requested an opinion from my HR representative prior to ordering business cards for my team, which improved the quality of our dialog, trust, and frequency of dialog. Don't wait until you need your HR representative to communicate.

One practice commonly found in IT is the mistrust of the HR group. This is unjustified in most cases. Furthermore, HR is typically involved too late. Human Resources can be a great ally to the IT Manager. Ally yourself with your HR representative. When I was faced with the termination of one of my Supervisors, my HR representative was invaluable in coaching me to say the right words to the Supervisor and protect the company from liability.

Build trust with your HR representative so that they willingly share with you when it can benefit you. If some activity is taking place that can affect your team, wouldn't you prefer to find out sooner than later?

Keep these points in mind and strive to make the correct decisions.

Success Strategies for Technology Management

Chapter 16

Your Contribution to the Corporation & the Corporation's Contribution to You

Keep your eye on the ball. Your goals must be aligned with the goals of the corporation (i.e.; the business). Let us generalize here and agree that all corporations exist to make a profit. Some do not, but these lessons still apply.

Technology may be your profession, but you exist to serve a larger organization—your business. Not everything you do will appear to enhance the organization (e.g., Data Backup, Disaster Recovery Planning, data base tuning, UPS testing), but many will. In any case, let nothing you do interfere with the goals of the corporation (e.g., making a profit).

When you are able to fulfill your primary goals such as those referenced above, you can remain invisible. Miss something, and you will gain recognition very quickly—undesirable recognition. If you remain invisible most of the time, garnering only unfavorable feedback, you are not doing your job. Manage your group efficiently and add value to the organization in ways discussed here, and your contributions will not go unnoticed. Let your goals not detract from the business, but actively contribute towards the goals of the business and not remain invisible.

Look for opportunities to join industry organizations to hear what other companies are doing with technology. Communicate what you are doing because other organizations may have experience with something you are doing and be able to offer insight that proves to be of great value to you.

Contribute, contribute, and contribute. You will be recognized. Recognition will not be financial at first, but you will gain respect. With respect comes trust. With trust, you will find that you will have the freedom to do more and find it less difficult to gain financial approvals. Thus you will have more opportunities to achieve great things. Your leaders will value your contributions to their organization. When your contributions are appreciated, you will be happier.

Ultimately you should begin to see the obvious financial perks such as salary increases, cash bonuses, stock options, etc.

You may have heard this many times before, but it is worth hearing again: "Don't worry about the money." Too many people do jobs strictly for the money, and not for personal satisfaction or fulfillment (e.g., self respect or happiness).

1. Keep your eye on the goal.
2. Do what you love, and love what you do.
3. The money will come.

You have to be passionate about what you're doing or you'll give up after the first setback. The more you love what you do the more you will persevere.

—Robert Pagliarini

Obstacles are those frightful things you see when you take your eyes off your goal.

—Hannah More

Value and integrity first! Love your work. It's all good!

Chapter 17

Stress and Your Job

Stress is a funny thing; you can never tell what will cause it in any one person. "Stressing Out" is, after-all, a self-inflicted condition. We often call events stressful, but the same event will create different reactions in different people, making stress completely relative. Once you see stress that way, you will begin to handle it better.

Technology, we all know, never works as well as it was designed to work, resulting in stress generating situations. Many people thrive on stress and appear to be very successful. There are many people that allow stress to consume their lives. Those people do not typically experience great levels of happiness or success. Understand that most people will stress out similarly no matter what the situation. Many people will completely stress out over the seemingly smallest of items while you will also witness people handling the worst situations with seemingly no stress at all.

Leaders become better at handling stress as events and circumstances have a greater impact on life and they begin to see how they are allowing stress generating events to alter their lives, or the lives they desire.

Anticipate the stress generating events and accept them through positive actions. For example, if one service you provide is critical to the business, have a backup plan for the inevitable technology failure. In this example, stress points out an opportunity for you to provide a better service. Your actions to address this opportunity will reduce stress when the breakage occurs. The technology may break down, but the service you provide to the business will not. The business will learn to trust that you are doing the right things in their best interest. Don't allow cost to stop you from providing outstanding service levels to the business when TCO and ROI are acceptable. Spending may not be questioned by the business if you have an established reputation for protecting their ability to conduct business using sound economic principles. If your area is audited, you should stand behind your spending with the confidence that you are doing what is right for the business at the best possible price. For these reasons, you should not get stressed out over an audit.

Chronic stress has a variety of negative side effects on individuals and on the team such as weight gain, increased risk of sickness, indecision and low energy levels, all causing lower productivity. For these reasons, leaders should improve their overall health and encourage good health in others. Proper daily exercise and good dietary practices should become second nature as should several of the activities suggested here.

Companies often have programs devised to address fitness. Many such programs are designed to be anonymous so employees feel confident that this reach for help will not be held against them. Try to get your people involved in company programs to improve health. Hopefully your company supports such employee initiatives in sponsored programs. Some involve diet while others involve physical fitness or a gym membership. Many companies have psychological aid programs to assist employees feeling stress to the point it becomes unhealthy. At the very least, your team will become educated about health and opportunities for personal improvements. At best, they will become healthier, happier and more productive. Obviously, the health of your people is not your responsibility. However, getting your people informed about, and encouraging involvement in company initiatives, is a leader's responsibility.

The ultimate objective to relieving stress is to remove or change the stressful thoughts. Do not permit the stress to dictate your feelings. If you can initiate changes to alleviate the stressful situation, do so. If you cannot initiate further change, you must conclude that your dwelling on the stressful event cannot improve it. Make a plan to disconnect from the cause of stress, document it, delegate it, and quit stressing over it. If contacting a Leader about an outage is essential, do it early to get it off your mind.

Never worry about things you cannot control, instead focus 100% on the important and urgent things in your life that you can impact, and achieve exceptional completion with them. If you cannot do anything about a situation, put the situation out of your mind because there may come a time later when you can make a difference and you can be ready. Recall the lesson we learned in a previous chapter; sometimes it is what it is and changing the situation is beyond your power. Utilize this thought to help sooth your mind: It is what it is. Accept what you cannot change and work around it, whether it be people or technology.

A lie creates stress. Tell the truth, no matter how painful. Pain from the truth will pass. Lying will likely bring more pain than telling the truth. A lie must be remembered and often times leads to more lying to cover the initial lie – all of which creates stress. Telling the truth may require significant courage, but you will feel good about yourself and build trust in your relationships – very powerful and good for you. The truth will truly set you free and permit you to move on to greater things while lying will keep your mind stuck in place as you continuously have to cover your tracks.

Be honest and tell the truth.

People (e.g.; customers) have their own goals and desires, often having no interest in cooperating with you, becoming difficult to work with. Review their situation and review your own situation carefully. Analyze what can be done (i.e.; what is possible). Be open—minded, accepting of new ideas and be honest. Help their situation where you can, remembering that *it is what it is.* Remembering this point can liberate you from a stressful situation brought on when a customer's demands exceed your capabilities.

Technology has limitations and can create tense situations. I can recall technology failures that would elevate my stress level so much that I would begin to feel lightheaded. At first I was amused, but an intense headache quickly brought me to the realization that this could not be healthy. I took a step back from the situation and took a deep breath so I was able to change my state of mind by simply acknowledging that this is the nature of the technology (*it is what it is*): *I have the best people working on it, and upon review of the situation, at a later time, we will develop a means of successful mitigation.* The next occurrence was handled much differently.

So once you determine that you have searched for, and seized opportunity, and cannot effect change at this time, how can you put work out of mind? Many leaders utilize different techniques, but all techniques involve occupying the mind with something else. Only you know what else can completely occupy your mind, disallowing any chance of the event creating stress and consuming you.

Appreciate where you are. Slow down and look around. We have a habit of constantly looking to the future, planning and preparing for things to come and forgetting to appreciate the present for all its wonderful gifts. Do not allow yourself to miss the beautiful things that the present has to offer because you are too busy checking your schedule, checking for messages or doing just one more thing on the never ending list of responsibilities.

[149]

Appreciate and relish who you are and where you are at each moment, or you can choose to feel stressed and fatigued by upcoming events, missing the present.

Suggested activities for redirecting your mind include:
- Physically remove yourself (i.e.; take a break)
- Direct your focus to other projects
- Restful meditation
- Music that can make you feel good
- Reading or writing
- Kids
- Hobbies
- Physical exercise (i.e.; join a gym)
- Charity work
- Sports
- Fishing (considered restful meditation by many.)
- A movie or TV
- Shopping
- Seeking professional assistance for wellness

Activities to be avoided include:
- Abusing alcohol or drugs
- Ignoring the situation
- Other destructive activities

Being physically active and eating healthy helps your body and mind to be better prepared for stress when it does find you. Sometimes stress worms its way into your psyche when you're not ready for it. If you are not involved in any of these suggested activities, you should make it a point to get involved. Call it 'me time' or 'family time' or 'unwind time' or 'stress blow-out time', but set time aside for it. Make it routine. That's what great leaders do.

Another method utilized for forgetting and de-stressing is to 'write it down and put it out of mind'. If on Friday you realize that you absolutely must get something done on Monday, do not stress over it. Instead; write it down, schedule time on your calendar; then forget about it until Monday with the confidence that you will see a reminder at the appropriate time and address it then. The review time may be a great time for you to seek out opportunity and effect change. You should leave yourself a message or reserve time on your Monday schedule. Methods were discussed in more detail in a previous chapter; "Get Organized".

So you have not seen a great Leader living a life that is completely free of work activities? They do exist. Those *individuals that work all the time cannot be very happy people and being ha*ppy is a basic component of being a great leader. In most cases, if the Leader is not happy, the team will not be happy (or willingly follow), and success will remain elusive.

So remember to find the cause of your stress, think about it in terms of your power and capability to change it (i.e.; opportunity). Now if everything is being done that can be done, and you can do nothing more, allow yourself to move on to something else where you can make a difference—a new activity, issue, whatever—with a plan to return to the stressful scenario in the future when circumstances have matured and you can make a difference.

Until you accept responsibility for the role you play in creating or maintaining your stress level, it will remain outside of your control. You can either change the situation or change your reaction. You should do a little of both. Since everyone has a unique response to stress, there is no "one size fits all" solution to managing it. No single method works for everyone or in every situation, so experiment with different techniques and strategies mentioned here or develop your own methods. Focus on what helps you feel calm and in control.

Remember and utilize the Serenity Prayer:
God, grant me the serenity to accept the things I cannot change, Courage to change the things I can, And wisdom to know the difference.

Chapter 18

Goals

Developing and setting goals is absolutely necessary for success because you cannot reach your destination until you know that destination. Furthermore, your goals must be known and understood by each member of your team.

Goals are defined by Encarta as something that you hope to achieve. It is the leader's responsibility to establish goals through knowing and understanding the business, the business practices, the technical environment and the IT support team. Goals must be developed to improve the business environment, educate your team, and improvement of the value of the technical environment.

A review of the environments should indicate areas that will benefit from improvements. If not immediately visible to you, meet with your team or meet with business constituents to determine what they like and don't like about the current environment.

For an example of how a technical solution not developed with constituents and disjoined from a business practice, can result in less than optimal results;

[153]

Reviewing and understanding the business impact of a large distribution center, my team agreed that the primary link required a backup so that the business would not suffer from a link or hardware outage. An outage would mean delayed shipments, fines, or lost business.

A cost effective link was installed that required operator intervention to activate. However, within months of implementation, the backup link proved to be inadequate to maintain normal business practices. Activation time was disruptive and link speed was inadequate. This revealed major gaps in the implemented backup solution.

The team was brought together for a strategy session to develop a new solution.

The routing protocol was changed and a permanent link was implemented for a faster backup route. The new routing protocol provided automated convergence after a failure, eliminating activation delays, and the permanent link provided the speed required for normal business operation.

The new solution was more costly, but provided the abilities the business required.

Once developed, establish goals by writing them down, either personally or in a regularly scheduled report to your boss. Your goals cannot be a secret. Once approved, and sometimes before approval, communicate your intentions; with your team, with peers, with your boss, and with constituents.

Utilize your team to develop goals and strategy, even when you are confident you require their input. You will require their commitments, in body and soul, so engage them at the start.

You will be expected to bring ideas for improvements to the organization. However, you do not operate alone and should rely on the entire IT team. Methods for developing your strategies include;

- Strategy Meetings
- Whiteboard sessions
- Presentation of graphical material (e.g.; Visio, PowerPoint)

In the interest of sharing and of ensuring all parties understand similarly; always follow up strategy meetings and whiteboard sessions with email that appropriately documents all discussion (e.g.; ideas, cost, time frames, personnel, business impact, technology, next steps).

Involve constituents in the business community as early as appropriate. Business managers need to be aware and are needed to support changes in their environment.

Once a project has been established, standard guidelines for effective project management must be followed.

Tools that can be utilized for sharing include;

- Office bulletin board postings
- email
- Internal web flashes

[155]

- Calendar entries for milestones and expectations (e.g.; completed server installation) where responsible project members are invited so the milestone appears on their calendars as well.

- Status meetings through standard project management processes

- Status meetings with your boss

- Impromptu meetings as new items develop worthy of discussion (include all appropriate parties; e.g.; technical team, IT peers, business constituents, other managers)

Chapter 19

Mentoring & Giving Back — Simple Rules for Daily Practice

Practice these mentoring rules daily to easily meet basic mentoring objectives and contribute to the enhancement of your life and the lives of the people you work with.

Mentoring Rule #1: You are not irreplaceable; nor should you want to be

Contrary to what you might have been taught, it should not be your goal to make yourself irreplaceable. In fact, your actions should indicate otherwise. There are many individuals qualified to do your job, but your company is grateful to have you because of your team approach and stellar results.

It is advisable for you always to have one or two people in your organization that could replace you if necessary. This should be viewed as mentoring. They must not only be qualified, but motivated. This point is not to be overlooked; I have been frustrated by people I have known to be qualified, but who are completely unwilling to comply with the demands of the role. Do not waste too much time mentoring this person to assume your position. You must be gently preparing someone to take the wheel and drive, making it possible for you to be promoted or moved comfortably. Knowing that your previous area is covered—effectively, the way that you would want it—is the best way to move.

You will form a personal bond with the person that you are mentoring. You wish for them to be successful, and you must do everything in your power to teach and show them how to be successful at their job. Their success becomes your success. As mentor, you must show them how to be successful in the ways that you have been successful. When they reach a level of success from which they can move into your position, you will have the freedom to move on, knowing that your area will be managed the way you would want it managed. Typically, leaders aren't found; rather, they are developed—by you—through mentoring.

Mentoring Rule #2: Your area must be a known entity

This refers to an understanding of your area by others that are impacted by your moving. Their understanding only increases your value. Documented processes and technology documentation are absolutely necessary for honest, well—intentioned transparency. Adherence to ITIL (Information Technology Infrastructure Library) standards will ensure that subsequent Leaders/Managers can understand and continue your legacy. Be proud of what you leave behind. Sharing knowledge and experiences with others is known as "giving back" to the IT organization— and, ultimately, to the entire company.

Take opportunities to educate other parts of the organization. Present installations, or technologies over which you preside, during *Learn—over—Lunch* sessions or something similarly approachable for you. This serves as *give—back*, and can only heighten your level of esteem within the organization. Hold a meeting for project closure that includes a colorful, exciting, and descriptive presentation illustrating the value of the new service. Invite Executives when appropriate.

You can further extend your practices, "giving back" to the business community as a whole, by speaking/presenting at industry functions (e.g.; trade shows, blog contributions, social media, and so forth).

Your company may be involved in civic *give—back* to the community through company—sponsored social activities. Sometimes a charity is favored by your company, so participate when you can. Think about involving your family, if at all possible. Set an example for your team to get them involved.

Share and teach.

Keep no secrets.

Respect all people.

Mentoring Rule #3: Respect to be respected

Give respect graciously and sincerely always. At the same time, you absolutely must achieve it for yourself. Don't expect respect from your organization until you demonstrate self respect and respect for others. Don't anticipate respect too quickly, because anything worthwhile take time. Know your job and do it well. Respect all others, and they will respect you in return. Respect for you will then spread like wildfire as it becomes the "right thing to do".

Without respect, you cannot fulfill your mission, no matter how knowledgeable and well—intentioned you are, or carefully planned the endeavor is. You require funding, time, and cooperation. You will not get these without respect.

Men are respectable only as they respect.

—Ralph Waldo Emerson

On a similar note, it is inadvisable to waste your energy on vengeance. Justice has a way of catching up with those that do bad things to others.

These basic rules are all enhanced by communication. They complement and build upon each other over time.

You should select a role model within your organization, your profession, in politics, in sports, or in movies. Role models should inspire and be a positive influence. A great Hollywood role model for me is Marshall Matt Dillon of *Gunsmoke*. He is strong and tough, but is also warm, honest, and friendly. His integrity inspires his friends to be great people, and he garners respect wherever he goes. His leadership principles include never to take friends for granted, and to show respect and compassion for all, while doing his job as best he can. He likes his friends, and his friends like him. He would do anything for them, and he trusts that they would do anything for him.

A wonderful example for trusting in your team can be found in a 1958 Gunsmoke episode called "The Killer". The sequence I reference can be seen as Gunsmoke "The Killer" Act 3 at http://www.youtube.com/watch?v=aqyojnM9tlc . It is a short (4:35) segment that should be viewed by all potential leaders.

If you are a Leader, several people may have already selected you as a role model. You may not know their identities, and you might not be able to mentor all of them, but you can mentor several individuals to different degrees. Choose carefully where your efforts are expended. Often you can simply mentor by setting an example of behavior. Your actions must benefit the person being mentored, the team, the larger organization, and, of course, yourself. Consider it an honor and a privilege, and take every opportunity to share your knowledge and experience.

Have an esteemed *right—hand person* or two, who, by virtue of their integrity and respect, will allow you to be out of the office for short periods (e.g.; vacations or trade shows) without being concerned about the ongoing operation of your area.

Mentoring Rule #4: Appreciate.

Leadership is a gift. You should be sincerely grateful that you are in a position of responsibility and respect, having the power to influence your own destiny.

Be grateful for the people that work for you, the people that are your team. They are there to help you succeed.

Be grateful for the business that utilizes your services to create market opportunities and maintain a healthy position of competitiveness in their market niche.

Be grateful for your executive leadership because they are there for you and will help you to be successful.

Appreciate your work, your abilities, and your value in the machine that is your business.

Appreciate industry organizations that exist for the benefit of your industry and your company.

Appreciate your IT peers throughout the world as they face many of the same challenges you face and resolve every day.

Appreciate technology for all that it could be and all that it could accomplish in your world.

Be grateful you are in a position to be a catalyst for change.

Appreciate your health and your ability to work and contribute every day.

Appreciate those who seek mentoring from you.

Appreciate those who take the time and care enough to mentor you.

Chapter 20

Planning

A fool with a plan can outsmart a genius with no plan.

—T. Boone Pickens

Imagine what a genius with a plan can do! You may not consider yourself a genius, but… arm yourself with a good plan, and great things can happen.

Always start with the goal in mind. Understand why a project or group of projects is needed, and what will be produced for the business. Project plans become sub—components of a strategic plan. Having plans is the single most important part of a strategy.

Evaluate risks, and be prepared to talk about risks and your plans for mitigation. Be prepared, and anticipate the questions that will come from business or financial representatives.

Plan for your personnel and for your environment. Make it a strategic plan that falls in line with larger strategic plans of the larger organization. Other Managers and Leaders will respect you more for having a plan.

Components of a strategic plan should include the following:

- ✓ Current and projected organization charts
- ✓ Risk management and mitigation
- ✓ Education plans and budgets
- ✓ Industry trade show participation with budgets
- ✓ Reward schedules and budgets
- ✓ Physical/Technical environment documentation (shows awareness)
- ✓ Anticipated or probable technical trends or changes in your organization (shows industry knowledge)
- ✓ Environment evolution (1, 3, or 5—year plan)
- ✓ Planned collaborators (internal and external)
- ✓ Annual budget projections
- ✓ Change projections impacting the business and how to approach them and communicate them to the business
- ✓ Communication method detail

There will be circumstances beyond your control that will force you to adjust your strategy from time to time. Be cautious about planning for changes outside your realm of responsibility. If the above list or level of detail is not appropriate for your situation, scale it up or down. The review of your plan with your team, and peers within your company, is encouraged. External review can also be beneficial. One suggestion for external review is a trusted vendor; another is a group of industry peers in similar companies; a third could be consultants, but these opinions will require payment. The opinions of consultant SMEs (Subject Matter Experts) can be of great value, and help support your proposal. The cost of an expert will be well worth it when you are planning something that could impact the entire corporation for years to come—thus, having a potentially great impact on your position and career.

Once you feel confident that your plan is complete, request to share it with the leadership. Provide your plan either by written report (with graphics and footnotes) or, preferably, by presentation (strongly recommended). A presentation is preferable and recommended because it guarantees a captive audience and it makes you immediately available for questions. Questions should be encouraged, because they are a very good sign your audience is interested. Present multiple graphics and pictures to keep things interesting. Be confident and passionate about your plan. You took the time to create it, research it, and have collaborated with your team and your peers. Given your intimate knowledge of the proposal, you should never read text for your presentation. You should be knowledgeable, passionate and confident about it. A lack of confidence will surely kill acceptance of your plan. Have printed copies of your presentation available, as they will likely be requested for later review.

For example:

I presented my strategic plan to a new CIO. The CIO was very interested with my entire presentation and asked questions. When I was done, he told me how impressed he was that I had a solid strategic plan with such detail. By providing this feedback, he was encouraging me and instilling a sense of loyalty.

Self—confidence begets respect. Respect allows you to execute your plans. Also think about this when you are in the audience for a proposal presentation. Participate by asking questions, respecting as you would want to be respected.

Make it your practice to document all that you do, ask your team to document what they do, and review their documentation together. Tracing the team's steps at a later date should be an easy task. If that is not the case, you could find yourself in trouble at a later date, scrambling to determine what was done during implementation.

You want to go home on time after a productive day and be able to relax; this is made possible by an organized, documented and well planned day.

Your job is your career. Your career is a large part of your life. Plan accordingly. Go forward with confidence, and conquer.

Satisfaction and happiness can be yours.

Chapter 21

Managing Teleworkers

"Teleworkers" in the technology profession are challenging, but completely manageable. Where a support position that does not require full—time, hands—on access to technology systems and the responsibilities of the job can be fulfilled with a suitable office space and an access link to office systems, opportunities for teleworking* from home abound. Conversely, the daily management and maintenance of operational technology (hardware) requires a daily presence of engineers; telework opportunities will be more limited, but not impossible. Like I once told a telephone technician on my team: *The telephones we maintain are in the office. How can we provide value to the company if when the phone system breaks we are not here to fix it?*

For example: the IT Service Desk has daily requirements that are typically not location dependant (in most organizations), so the Service Desk is one IT support team that is able to fulfill their obligations regardless of location (i.e., the nature of the responsibilities of the IT Service Desk do not require the associates to be anywhere in particular, however, separation presents new challenges). Furthermore, working from home is a powerful incentive for commitment and loyalty to your company; for retaining high quality staff. Be cautious to maintain immediate communication for associates since office items such as electronic bulletin boards with up—to—the—minute ticket status will not be viewable by teleworkers. Ideally, teleworking associates need pop—up windows when ticket status changes and they usually need immediate access to other IT associates via Instant Messaging.

Other technology areas that can benefit from having associates telework include application development and programming, server operating—system support (e.g., patch management, security administration, and user administration). There are still other technology support areas that can benefit from teleworking such as application support or email support. Unfortunately, for most IT hardware support groups, opportunities are somewhat limited for teleworking since engineers need to have access to hardware for hands-on adjustments or repairs. This requires presence in the office, as nonattendance could result in extended outages that will affect the business. However, telework opportunities can be found.

Even for the hands-on hardware engineers, you will find opportunities for teleworking, provided these engineers have work they can perform remotely. For teams of four or more engineers, consider splitting employee time between their homes and the office, providing for some level of local support, while offering the incentives that working from home brings. When splitting time between home and the office, ensure that engineers are always present in the office to provide hands—on support, while other engineers will have the opportunity to intermittently telework via secure remote—access technologies. Secure remote—access can provide administrative access to hardware devices, allowing engineers to fine tune hardware parameters remotely.

An opportunity / benefit that should not be dismissed is that of a tele-worker's value in a disaster scenario. When company facilities are not available, you have a pre-tested tele-worker to fall back on. Include this function in your disaster readiness testing.

It is best to occasionally have engineers working side by side in the office (e.g., one engineer teleworks Monday and Tuesday, while the other teleworks Thursday and Friday; shared time in the office

Team of Four "in-the-office" Schedule						
WEEK START DATE	Monday	Tuesday	Wednesday	Thursday	Friday	Weekend Emergency Phone Coverage
1-Aug	John	John	John			John
	Sally	Sally	Sally			
			Jane	Jane	Jane	
			Fred	Fred	Fred	
8-Aug			John	John	John	
			Sally	Sally	Sally	Sally
	Jane	Jane	Jane			
	Fred	Fred	Fred			
15-Aug	John	John	John			
	Sally	Sally	Sally			
			Jane	Jane	Jane	Jane
			Fred	Fred	Fred	
22-Aug			John	John	John	
			Sally	Sally	Sally	
	Jane	Jane	Jane			
	Fred	Fred	Fred			Fred

Example of an office coverage schedule, team of four, splitting time

mid—week works well, and provides for full, technical, hands—on coverage 5 days per week). Creating the office space for such an arrangement could be challenging so plan accordingly. Have a contingency plan for those days on which your on—site engineer calls out due to illness. For this reason, I recommend this strategy for teams of four or more, having at least two engineers in the office on any day.

Where teams of one exist in your organization, you will need to become more creative utilizing regular communication. There will be opportunities for you to have teleworkers in the office for department events (e.g., "town-hall" meetings, awards presentations, technology presentations, vendor meetings, education). For those on your team that rarely visit the office, you need to encourage regular team communication through technologies such as:

- Instant messaging
- Text messaging
- Audio conferencing
- Video conferencing
- Email

Telework needs to be assigned (i.e., each teleworker will necessarily have tasks to do remotely). There may be work tasks coming in from other IT groups (e.g.; problem investigation and correction) or from the user community (e.g., database search modification requests, testing).

These activities must be tracked. Utilizing an online request system or utilizing email to create a record of a user's change request may be sufficient in your environment. Documented communication is important.

A policy must be created and shared with Tele-workers so that your expectations for the telework environment are shared and known. A sample of general concerns for a telework policy is shown here. Review this example and integrate the best points into your own telework policy*.

Additionally, record the address or addresses where telework will be performed with details regarding access and deliveries.

Through casual or official verbal, face-to-face communication with your customers, determine how your teleworkers are satisfying their customers. The communication with customers should be verbal and not rely solely on email or other messaging techniques. Let your teleworkers know about feedback from their customers — particularly positive feedback about exemplary performance.

For example: *While I was speaking with customer John yesterday, he mentioned how much he appreciates your work.* This encourages future exemplary performance. These are valuable individuals on your team. Guide them to become greater team contributors by keeping them informed, involved and inspired.

Having teams geographically dispersed presents many new challenges for the IT Manager since company funds cannot be squandered on travel expense and lodging to bring teams together

---

Teleworker General Guidelines

- Define qualifications for teleworking
- Define the physical attributes for the telework space
- Define company safety standards for the telework space
- Define what equipment the telework space will consist of
- Define what equipment the company will provide
- Define teleworker responsibilities for equipment and maintain a complete inventory
- Define what equipment the teleworker must provide
- Define procedures for technical assistance in the event of a telework disruption
- Define the teleworker daily schedule
- Communicate the teleworker daily schedule to all members of the team
- Define expectations for telework in an emergency such as Disaster Recovery
- Define technologies that will be used to maintain contact (e.g.; phone, SMS, email)
- Define your expectations for availability (e.g.; days and hours of availability)
- Define how a telework agreement will be terminated

---

on a frequent basis. For those cases, once or twice per year will be the limit. Unity and shared focus are still required, which signifies that your team and your people need to communicate and interact in order to perpetuate team harmony. Make use of the items listed above to communicate regularly. Regularly scheduled team meetings, facilitated externally (audio conference calls or video conferencing) will be acceptable for these situations.

Unifying geographically disperse teams presents an even greater leadership challenge. In this relatively new endeavor, a Manager will need to lead in ways not taught in years past.

The first challenge you need to undertake is to ensure teleworkers have a sense of purpose and understand the role they play in the overall success of the team. They need to have their value reinforced by their Manager from time to time.

Another important challenge is ensuring that environment knowledge and information is distributed and shared adequately for teleworkers. Things that an associate would normally be exposed to daily in an office environment will need greater attention to make certain that the information reaches associates who are teleworking.

These items include but are not limited to:

- Project issues and operational turnover
- Technology environment information (e.g.; documentation posters they may not have access to)
- Status meeting output
- Change request meeting output (e.g.; application, network, PC image changes that affect users calling the IT Service Desk*)
- Personnel changes

Distributing weekly change reports, personnel changes, or technical—environment information electronically will help maximize efficiency. Typically, you must depend upon instructions being distributed in this way to assure consistent interpretation of content. Electronic mail deliveries may need to be followed by an Instant Message or other communication to each individual teleworker, to confirm that the material was received and it is fully understood. Instant messaging is a simple way to quickly communicate with someone. This responsibility will easily overwhelm a Manager that has multiple teleworkers, so assigning a helper of your choice (e.g., Manager, supervisor, lead engineer), or creating a rotational assignment for the team is recommended so you are not overwhelmed.

Delegating this assignment does not eliminate the leader's responsibility to communicate with each individual on a regular basis. As with any team, the Leader is required to maintain a cohesive group with a particular set of goals that are clearly understood by everyone on the team. This responsibility does not change when team members become teleworkers. However, the responsibility becomes more challenging, and will require greater time and effort. There will be team members that require very little management and one—on—one communication, while others will perform much better when they receive regular communications and guidance from their Manager. Do not fight these needs, but satisfy them as best you can to ensure this person's continued commitment and loyalty to you and your goals. Conversely, do not over—communicate with strong team members that work very well with minimal supervision and whom interact regularly with the team. You do not want to be seen as overbearing or displaying little confidence in the teleworker.

If there are only a couple people on your team teleworking on any given day, consider making the communication yourself. The information has more significance coming from the Manager. Manage your time to be as effective as you can be. Instant messaging is quick and easy.

In addition to your Telework Guidelines, provide access to education tutorials that teach teleworkers how they are expected to work, how to set up and utilize the equipment, how to obtain technical support. If any of these items do not exist in your environment, engage the correct managers to get them in place, including your HR representative. If expectations are not set for management and the teleworker, results will be unpredictable, based on each individual's honesty and work ethic. Ensure the material provided matches your expectations by viewing it to approve or disapprove it.

I have referenced how making your job "personal" is something that a Leader must do. Since you will not share space with each teleworker on a daily basis, you must make it your mission to spend some amount of time with everyone on the team—working remotely or working in the office. Even when an individual on your team spends only one day per week teleworking, you will want to apportion time to communicate with that person about their day, to help maintain a healthy flow of information in both directions using the methods listed above (i.e., You need to know what your people are doing, and they need to know what is happening within the technical environment at the office). Such technologies as Instant Messaging help to ensure home workers will be active parts of your team, and are less intrusive on a person's busy work schedule than a visit or a phone call. As for verbal communication; you will see that casual may be best, but some personalities will require a formally, scheduled time.

[177]

As the Leader, you must make yourself available regularly by utilizing a presence technique that will ensure you are easy to find and contact, creating confidence among your remote team that you are available. Presence technology can help people find you at all times. Remote workers cannot simply walk over to your office or retrieve you from a meeting when they urgently need to speak with you regarding a critical support issue, so make yourself, or a significant aid, easily reachable. Have an alternate contact or two available in an escalation list shared amongst your team.

The escalation list should include:
1. You
2. Your backup person (a Manager, Supervisor, or Lead Engineer)
3. A group number to call
4. The IT Service Desk*
5. An administrative assistant

Make sure people know when it's okay to shut down and unplug from work. Unnecessary stress or burnout can occur when people feel they can never stop working. You need to foster an environment that promotes a work—life balance, not a sense the teleworker is chained to a desk and a network connection. Without a bus, a train, or traffic to beat, a teleworker does not have the normal incentive to stop work for the day and may work excessive hours.

Additionally, people with Teleworker capabilities and practice will prove to be of great value in disaster recovery scenarios where system access can be made available as part of the recovery service. Simply point Teleworkers to the new systems and they can be up and in business relatively quickly.

Strategy and policies regarding disaster recovery should be published, known, understood, and practiced so that there is no confusion during an actual event.

The lessons, as in all team lessons that are provided here:

- Treat teleworkers as significant and vital parts of your team.
- Teleworkers require increased efforts in communication.
- Communicate with teleworkers regularly to keep them engaged and contributing to your team's objectives.
- Provide inspiration, keeping motivation strong and morale high.
- Encourage your local team to engage teleworkers whenever they can.
- Gage a teleworker's needs for supervision and communicate accordingly.
- Working from home is a privilege that you offer — not an obligation.

---

*IT Service Desk:

The IT Service Desk (a.k.a. Help Desk*) is a component of the Information Technology Infrastructure Library and is the single point of contact between service providers and users. A typical Service Desk manages incidents and service requests, also handling user communication.*

Best Management Practices: retrieved May, 2011 from

http://www.best—management—practice.com/gempdf/ITIL_Glossary_V3_1_24.pdf

*Teleworking as defined by the state of North Carolina:

This arrangement brings the work to the worker. Often it is not a full work week, but a few days where the employee can work without the interruptions of the office. Teleworking a few days each week has proven to increase productivity in many instances.

Not everyone is right for teleworking —— it takes a certain type of employee to be a successful teleworker. For example they may be required to share a central office space on days when working in the office. From the management perspective, it takes an individual willing to trust employees to be productive without constant direct supervision.

When the right fit of teleworker and manager is found, the benefits are numerous.

North Carolina State Government: retrieved July 25, 2011 from

http://teleworking.osp.state.nc.us/wahtis.htm

*Tele-work Policy as defined by the State of California:

This policy defines expectations for environment, information security, equipment, health and safety. You should also include expected working hours. Department of Personnel Administration: retrieved

July 29, 2011 from *http://www.dpa.ca.gov/dpa-info/telework/environment.htm*

Tele-working Policy examples from the Telework Research Network can be found online at
http://www.teleworkresearchnetwork.com/sample-documents/telecommuting-policy-sample

Success Strategies for Technology Management

Chapter 22

Basic IT Infrastructure Design Steps for Corporate IT Leaders & Enterprise Architects

This chapter was written to provide the basic, necessary actions and positions for IT Architects, managers and leaders. It requires a pragmatic mindset, and should remain simple for success to be realized. Always remember to practice the K.I.S.S. philosophy (Keep it Simple, Stupid!). Unnecessary complexities usually result in waste (e.g., miscommunication, misunderstanding, wasted time, resources, effort, and money). Consider that the shortest distance between two points is a straight line; in most cases, the best plan is the simplest one.

If you feel that you already know the business, but have not taken and expanded upon the following basic steps, you are setting yourself up for failure.

As you know, problems will find you. Every problem should be viewed as an opportunity to introduce positive change. Every problem has a solution. You just need to develop it. To every question, ask *why?* To every answer, ask *why?* Only by asking over and over, will you find the correct solution.

A pessimist sees the difficulty in every opportunity; an optimist sees the opportunity in every difficulty.

—Winston Churchill

A *corporation*, in the simplest terms, is people working together to make money. Your goal should be to find ways to help the business make money. Working together is the key component. What exactly do business people need to do with each other, and how can they do it? What is possible? Does it include talking, messaging, applications, sales, order entry, customer service, social networking, inventory, distribution, delivery? Imagine yourself as the savior of the business. It sounds simple, but you can bet that it doesn't happen overnight. If at first you don't succeed, move on to the next opportunity, and revisit that other one later, when people, the business, the technology, and/or attitudes have changed. Don't obsess about the past and expend too much energy on an event that cannot be redone or undone.

You are the technologist, aren't you? Become a team player with the business—a team born to develop solutions for making money. Become recognized and accepted as the technology expert on the business team (e.g.; the network expert; the mobility expert; the sales processing expert; the data warehouse expert). Technology is always changing; is business changing with it? This is precisely where you, the IT professional, can provide value to the business. If business issues or opportunities are outside your area, involve the appropriate Manager. They will likely be grateful that you have identified a need and contacted them about it. If they choose not to act, you can escalate, but it may be better to leave things be so that you do not irreparably damage your relationship with this manager. Choose wisely and tread lightly.

Where you have to work with multiple business units or divisions, you must select the unit where you will start. I have always used three prioritized criteria:

1. Determine where the company has decided to focus its financial resources to the advantage of a particular business or businesses.

2. Determine which business unit contributes most to company revenue and success, or can greatly influence company revenue based on technology advancements.

3. Lastly, and you will find this unavoidable; Determine if there is a business unit that voices their concerns loudest and is likely to influence the organization's opinion of you — good or bad, accurate or not. This may be an opportunity for you to turn a negative situation into a positive, revenue generating environment.

Your attention may need to go to a back office unit that supports the business (e.g.; Customer Service; Finance; Accounts Payable). In that case, you must prioritize based upon that unit's ability to affect your success and reputation. This will typically align well with company goals.

After you have selected a business unit, speak with your boss and peers about it. They may have experience with this unit and can provide valuable input. You will need to work with multiple business units concurrently. Do not over—commit, but anything less than a 100% commitment will be unacceptable. Like them, you have limited resources. You can offer alternatives such as contract employees or public cloud services, but be sure to specify costs — even estimates.

Create a list of business units and contacts that you will investigate. Prioritize the list based on the criteria of the bullets above.

> *One morning I found myself with limited technical resources and multiple outages. My engineers worked on two of the outages while the third would have to wait. The first two outages were business units. One unit was able to quantify downtime in dollars. The third outage was the Finance Group. The Finance Group could scream the loudest and the business units experiencing outages were familiar with this fact. However, a quick phone call to the Finance Group representative was all that was needed. I explained the situation and that I was addressing the issues before me in a priority that was best for the company. My point was understood and taken well. I then placed calls to the other two units and explained how I had prioritized their outages and what actions we were taking to make corrections and get them back to work. Everybody was satisfied (i.e.; Win—Win).*

> *After all three outages were corrected, I phoned the first two Managers and left messages that all systems should be functioning and they should call for any further issues. I could easily walk upstairs to the Finance Director, so*

I did. Direct, face—to—face communication was more personal and effective than a phone call. I thanked her for her understanding and cooperation and explained how the outage was corrected.

This experience allowed me to communicate with these business units and build upon my reputation. By visiting the Finance Director, I was able to gain a friend and supporter.

Learn the mission of the business. Study the established mission statement and the business architecture. Typically, businesses will spend much time and effort creating a Mission Statement that abstractly reflects the goals of the business, only to be ignored promptly by all. Don't ignore the Mission Statement— use it, instead, to gain an understanding of the business's goals.

Is there a business Mission Statement available? Is it meaningful to you? Speak with business leaders. Establish an ongoing dialogue. Develop allies. Be visible by appearing from time to time in places where business is conducted. Determine how the business is executing their mission. Determine how the business provides value to the customer. Prepare questions for these items, without making assumptions. If you do make assumptions, be sure to have them validated by the right business people in the organization.

Once you understand the mission of the business, you can apply your technology intelligence by asking yourself the following questions:

- Can technology be applied to benefit, improve, or change the business processes to make the business faster, cheaper, and easier?

- Can technology be used to improve the business customer's experience?

- What new developments in technology can be applied?

With the Internet, research is easy to do, so use it. Most vendors offer some form of free education on the Internet that can be accessed to familiarize you with a new technology or new challenges facing many businesses. Some will be video blogs, while others will be White Papers or Webinars. Their intention is to sell more products, but they typically mask that intention by keeping the content of the material more generic than product—specific (some more so than others). Any of the available methods typically take less than an hour of your time and tend to be very valuable for learning something new. Search the Internet for technology reviews or case studies, or simply ask your account representative, how to find free education about the technology they are selling.

How well do you know the environment from a business standpoint and a technology standpoint? You need to know where you are, because if you don't honestly know where you are when you start an improvement initiative, then you cannot possibly devise a plan to get where you want to be. You will have a seemingly productive, but excessively expensive, experience—a lot of actions with less—than—optimal results. So, make sure you know your environment.

You must put yourself in a position to be a catalyst for positive change.

High—level steps for a significant IT project:

1. Learn the business and technology environments and participants to understand the way things are.

2. Develop a VISION for the future.
   - From the information that you have gathered and your own knowledge of what is technologically possible, analyze the situation and develop an end—state VISION. A VISION is a future state that is superior to the current state.
   - Is your vision accurate or feasible? Ask the right business leaders to validate the vision you have developed. Engage other Technology Managers as appropriate.
   - Communicate!

3. IDENTIFY THE GAPS that exist between the current environment and the vision you have developed.
   - Can the vision be supported by current IT support staff? Can the support staff be supplemented?
   - Can we get from where we are today to the VISION?
   - What will the cost be? Will the business support the cost?
   - What will the timeframe be? How does the timeframe affect ROI?
   - What will be the success indicators that can be measured and reported (ROI)? Measure your results.

- What tools are needed?
- Review maintenance options and costs (TCO). When and how often should it be measured? Communicate all measurements with the business—good or bad.
- Communicate!

4. DEVELOP A PLAN to address the gaps you have identified.
   - Develop the new Enterprise architecture to fill the gaps.
   - Acquire the necessary tools.
   - Foster internal partnerships (e.g., business users and executives) with constituents that require success (i.e., have skin in the game).
   - List external requirements for:
     a. Talent
     b. Services
     c. Hardware
   - Build external collaborations as required with:
     a. Vendors
     b. Consultants
     c. Industry Organizations
   - Create an education schedule for staff (IT & business) as necessary.
   - Build measurements and assign an Availability Manager* to continually measure results (if you do not measure results and make adjustments, there will be waste).
   - Share the plan (Communicate).
   - Report measurements to the business (Communicate).

- Never underestimate the value of getting it right the first time.
- Plan your resources.
  - Business processes (anticipated measurable impact)
  - Resource utilization (internal & external)
  - Detailed budgets (measurable ROI & TCO)
  - Time line (Project Plan with measurable Milestones)
- Communicate!

5. PILOT the solution.
   - Select a small group of users to test the solution.
   - It is far better to discover unanticipated issues prior to production rollouts than afterward, when issues have a negative impact on business.
   - Before moving forward with implementation, write up the results of the pilot program and review it with IT and business representatives in a "post–pilot" meeting.
   - Communicate!

6. EXECUTE the plan (Implementation).
   - Establish documentation and the Service Catalogue Manager* (organize and communicate).
   - Establish Operational procedures and identify a Process Manager* to ensure that appropriate documentation is created and assigned to the right person or maintenance team for operational stability (organize and communicate).

- Assign a Service Continuity Manager* to evaluate risks that could impact the new service (due diligence) and create reactionary plans (organize and prepare).

- Assign a person to manage any incidents that occur during operation (i.e.; Incident management*) such as a senior service desk associate or a dedicated client manager.

- Communicate!

7. REVIEW

- Review what you have completed to determine if you have met your commitments.

- Upon completion, arrange a schedule with the business to re—take measurements and establish methods for regular, ongoing communications.

- Communicate utilizing written reports (status, changes, documentation, business feedback, TCO, ROI, etc.), email, meetings, phone calls, et al.

First learn the present processes and goals, then create a vision, and develop a plan to make the vision a reality, because when you act without knowing your goal, disaster strikes.

Vision without action is a daydream. Action without vision is a nightmare.

—Japanese Proverb

In any plan, you should be watching for functional single points of failure, whether they are borne of technology or process, and designing mitigation for them.

Technology failures are inevitable, so count on failures occurring at the very worst time. Anticipate failures and build in contingencies so the business can continue to operate. You don't want to be responsible for inhibiting the money—making machine.

Do not think in technological terms, but think in terms of business function. The business is utilizing technology *xyz*. What if it breaks? Design and implement an alternate technology to be in place and ready to go if needed. Ensure that the failure will be as transparent to the business as possible.

Discuss this with your implementation team, and include business people in your discussions when appropriate. Be honest about risks, and communicate any technology contingencies as well as business contingencies.

The business has been made aware of the risk/issue. Does the business have a plan for continuing operations, or does the responsibility befall you? Open and honest communication is strongly advised in order to avoid consequences later when the inevitable failure occurs.

This contingency planning activity is best when thought out and discussed in advance of a purchase, pilot or implementation. In some cases, the business will want to be involved in the discussion; at other times they will not. You should insist that they be aware of all risks and contingencies when moving forward — even when they elect not to participate in discussions. Communicate simply and effectively.

[193]

Your daily mode of operation should be one of regular review. The only constant in this world is change, and this is particularly true in technology. Your goal should be one of continuous improvement. You will never reach a final destination, and if you are not improving, then you are not providing value to your organization? Provide value through continuous improvement.

1. Observe and learn
2. Develop a vision
3. Identify gaps
4. Develop a plan
5. Pilot
6. Execute
7. Review, Measure & Report

I was once asked what is stressful about the IT leader's role. I replied, "Technology never works the way the salesman said it would." It rarely does, so plan accordingly.

Remain current regarding technology by subscribing to publications or online newsletters. Scan them daily for interesting subjects that might pertain to your responsibilities. Maintain dialogs with peers outside your organization and with industry groups regarding their pursuits.

Regularly re—evaluate the solutions you have implemented. Businesses change and technology evolves. What the team has found to be most effective this year may not be as effective in one to three years. Complacency breeds failure. Don't wait for bad things to happen. Always remember how important your team is to your success and give attention as necessary. Being more hands on, your team will recognize opportunities that you miss, so always be listening.

Remember that a fast application or network is better than slow, but slow is almost always better than down. Design contingencies accordingly.

Be careful to watch ROI and be mindful of business impact before suggesting another technology change. Be cautious of change for the sake of change. Alienating the business could be fatal.

SYNOPSIS:

Steps to determine what needs to be done:

1. This is where we are. (Demonstrates knowledge)
2. This is where we need to be. (Demonstrates vision)
3. These are the reasons we are not there. (Prioritizes documentation)
4. This is how we get there. (Demonstrates expertise)
5. These are the changes we should anticipate. (Demonstrates analysis)
6. These are the benefits and risks to the business and how they will be mitigated. (Demonstrates responsible planning)
7. Communicate and take action (Demonstrates courage to act)

———————————

*ITIL

The Information Technology Infrastructure Library was developed in 1988 by the UK government, to provide guidelines and specifications for IT services operations and management. ITIL is the most widely adopted approach for IT Service Management in the world. It provides a framework for identifying, planning, delivering, and supporting IT services to the business.
Definition retrieved May, 2011 from
http://www.itil—officialsite.com/AboutITIL/WhatisITIL.aspx

*Availability Manager

The Availability Manager is responsible for defining, analyzing, planning, measuring, and improving all aspects of the availability of IT services. The Availability Manager is responsible for ensuring that all IT infrastructure, processes, tools, roles, etc. are appropriate for the agreed service—level targets for availability.
Definition retrieved May, 2011 from
http://www.cmg.org/measureit/issues/mit33/m_33_1.html

*Incident Management

An 'Incident' is any event which is not part of the standard operation of the service and which causes, or may cause, an interruption or a reduction of the quality of the service.
The objective of Incident Management is to restore normal operations as quickly as possible with the least possible impact on either the business or the user, at a cost—effective price.
Definition retrieved July, 2011 from
http://www.itlibrary.org/index.php?page=Incident_Management

*Process Manager

The Process Manager is responsible for operational management of a process. The Process Manager's responsibilities include planning and coordination of all activities required to perform, monitor, and report the process (e.g., Change—Management Process).

Definition retrieved May, 2011 from

http://www.best—management—practice.com/gempdf/ITIL_Glossary_V3_1_24.pdf

*Service—Catalog Manager

The Service Catalogue is simply a repository of standard services that are available to business users from internal or external providers of IT services. The end—to—end management of the service catalogue lies in the hands of a Service—Catalogue Manager.

Definition retrieved May, 2011 from

http://www.forrester.com/rb/Research/role_overview_service_catalog_Manager/q/id/54565/t/2

*Service—Continuity Manager

The Service—Continuity Manager is responsible for ensuring that all services can be recovered in line with their agreed business requirements and timescales.

Definition retrieved May, 2011 from

http://www.best—management—practice.com/gempdf/itSMF_An_Introductory_Overview_of_ITIL_V3.pdf

Individuals with existing roles can hold multiple ITIL responsibilities.

[197]

Chapter 23

Negotiating with Vendors

Consider large purchases as opportunities to leverage an external resource. When negotiating, it is best to be in a position of strength. Strength will be relative to:

- Your company's size
- Your company's media exposure
- The vendor's size (i.e., flexibility)
- The amount of money to be exchanged
- The vendor's installed base in your company
- Installed base in all the vendor's accounts
- The vendor's relationship with your company and industry
- The details of the vendor's offer (i.e., what benefits do they provide?)
- More

Benefits can be abundant for both parties, so be aware of the pros and cons of each negotiating party. Your position will reveal opportunities for you to exploit your own strengths relative to the opportunities for both you and the vendor to benefit financially from the relationship. Do your homework and learn what is important to the vendor. This will prepare you to identify the opportunities, so that you know their negotiating benefits.

Relationship benefits for the vendor	Relationship benefits for your company
Building a new relationship for future opportunities	A new relationship bringing new opportunities to partner and learn through education and staff enhancement
Media exposure opportunities for successful integration with a new customer	Enhanced business activity generating new revenue or reducing the cost of existing revenue
Charity partnering opportunities	Charity partnering opportunities
Growth and Profit (i.e.; dollars and cents)	Competitive pricing A reliable solution Success

Table of benefits for comparison (create your own)

Negotiations are between people who are in this together, so it is crucial that you understand the person across the table. When you meet, provide a pleasant greeting (*Good morning!*), offer a chair, and offer coffee. The atmosphere is similar to that of a job interview. Look at the person non—invasively, but directly in the eye—can you trust them? Are they working toward a situation that benefits both parties equally? See beyond monetary concerns to build a mutually beneficial relationship, because dollars and cents are several steps below the most important components of the relationship as listed in the table above.

Put your emotions aside for negotiations. Trust is personal, but in the end, this arrangement is a business deal in which emotions can distort the truth. So, until the deal is done, leave emotion out of your decisions.

You must maintain a positive attitude while exploiting your own position of strength. As a customer, you always have the prerogative to seek alternative suppliers, and you should exercise that privilege. Ensure that you have the option of working with alternative suppliers.

For example:

> *Telecommunication carriers offer commodity services. There are several service providers that can effectively carry your company's communications. Take advantage of this situation by having two or more carriers providing services to your company. They will be aware of each other's presence in the account and will understand that their position in the account, even though viewed and treated as a partnership, is still a competitive environment. They will need to put their repeated best efforts into the account regarding service, pricing, and in media.*

Other providers will present you with restrictions around which you must navigate. For example, if all of your Database Administrators are skilled at maintaining a proprietary database solution, then you will not have the option of using another database product.

In those cases, leverage other aspects of the relationship. Exploit the relationship in the media, or demonstrate that the vendor will benefit from the relationship in the media. Negotiation will not necessarily bring you the lowest price possible; however, as long as the pricing provided is competitive in the current market, you need not concern yourself. The vendor has a strong position of negotiation and knows it, so will only give as much as required to keep the account through negotiations. This will place limits on what you can hope to gain in negotiations (e.g., pricing discounts, free services). However, your position remains strong because you are the customer, and you are providing revenue for this vendor. Trust that the sales representative does not wish to be the person who loses the account. Be strong and confident in your position, but not overly demanding with requirements or conditions.

With established vendor relationships in which there is installed base in your company, be wary of insisting on the lowest price available, because not only are you unlikely to receive it, but you can also damage the relationship, inhibiting the support advantages you should expect. If the relationship is more of a desirable type of 'partnership', consider the vendor to be a partner with conditions (i.e., make it known that this relationship exists and is maintained under certain expectations that must be honored by the vendor).

There are situations where competing resellers can be leveraged to obtain competitive bids for the same solutions. This approach is common when purchasing hardware, such as Wintel servers or network switches, and is strongly recommended whenever it is possible. It allows you to maintain a strong relationship with the manufacturer, while negotiating for the best price with Value—Added Resellers (VARs).

You will find that most service providers with a long—term, established business relationship with your company will no longer be providing competitive pricing. For this reason, you must occasionally obtain competitive bidding from competing vendors. You will have three optional courses of action:

1. Negotiate lower, competitive pricing.
When competitive bids are significantly lower, use them to negotiate better pricing from the incumbent provider.

2. Switch providers/vendors.
If the incumbent vendor refuses to meet your price—adjustment requests, evaluate the cost to replace the incumbent vendor with the competing vendor (ROI). The vendor challenging for the business will be in a position to provide certain conversion services free of charge. Negotiate whatever free services you can (e.g., waived installation charges).

3. Leave the situation as it is.
When existing pricing is competitive and the incumbent is providing adequate service for your business, the ROI calculations for acquiring a challenger's service may prohibit a change. The risks to the business and extra work for your staff may also make a change prohibitive.

All negotiations must have a win—win end result for all parties involved. If your victory is too one—sided, then you risk the loss of vendor aid and cooperation, turning a productive partnership into a shaky relationship that is not acceptably profitable for the vendor. If the vendor wins significantly, causing you regret, you will be compelled to search for a new supplier. Vendors are smart about this; they will not be attempting to win to such a degree that you feel you have lost. The vendor will be negotiating for win—win also.

The Encarta Dictionary defines *win—win* as *a situation in which all parties benefit in some way.* The situation is one in which everyone benefits.

Honesty always works best, and sincerity makes personal interaction more pleasant. When you need to end a relationship, honesty, and professionalism will be the best approach for doing so.

Enjoy the process. Negotiations are not a battle, but a process of building a winning situation and beneficial relationship for everybody.

Chapter 24

You are in a New Management Position? What to Do First: A 90—Day Plan

With a new position, you need to get started immediately, because you know that everyone is watching and waiting to see if you can do the job. This chapter will provide some guidance on where to concentrate your efforts for the first ninety days.

You can only make a first impression once. The first impression that you make is going to be the image that defines you for months to come, so dress for success, speak clearly, listen attentively, and be wary of using humor too soon as a method to break the ice or lighten the mood. Humor can be misinterpreted at this early stage of establishing your reputation at a new job. Humor is best left for established professional relationships; even then, always keep the humor clean, and not sexist, racist, ignorant or rude. These first three months will be critical to establishing your reputation (i.e., who you will be and how you will do things). Any misinterpretation of your intentions at this point could be fatal to your relationship with this person or take months to repair.

A new position is a new opportunity to start again and establish yourself as the Leader that you see yourself becoming. At this point, envision the Leader who you want to be, and nothing less. Be that person. Peers and subordinates will likely have pre—existing notions of who you are to be. Do not allow these influences to change who you really are. This is your new opportunity to do great things and to make a difference, professionally and personally.

Step one will be a combination of several activities since we usually don't have the luxury of focusing on one item at a time, covering several areas sequentially. Plan on executing simultaneously, expending more effort on the items that indicate to you, that they require more attention. You should be able to identify them in the first few weeks.

Create some personal space for yourself at the office. It will help ease the adjustment to a new environment. Include a family picture or a favorite desk lamp that helps you feel more at peace.

Your brain must be set in learning mode because you are not directing yet. You will need to learn the environment, the IT landscape and the people involved before you can start to provide direction. Providing direction too early will alienate you and delay you from gaining respect as a leader. The people on your team are your highest priority, so learn about them as soon as possible. When your new Leader expects you to "hit the ground running", beware not to attempt execution before obtaining the necessary background knowledge. If pressure from your Leader leads you to fail, you have only yourself to blame. Your Leader will likely not accept blame for this early failure.

People you will meet must include, among others: company leaders, department leaders, peers, your technical team and business constituents. Learn how all these people and teams interact. You may find it helpful to obtain a department organization chart. However, it will be a better learning experience for you to draw up your own organization chart as you familiarize yourself with the organization, just confirm its accuracy. A good, neutral person to help you with this exercise is a savvy Administrative Assistant. They are usually happy to share their knowledge and help new people get acclimated to the new environment. They may also be able to help you understand how your team interacts with the business. Get out of your office and meet people.

Once you have identified your team and your peers, learn who your incumbent vendors are and reach out to your vendor representatives, for the purpose of both identifying yourself and arranging to meet to discuss their relationships in your business, as well as to set your expectations for them.

Seek out as much technical—environment documentation as you can find, and study it. Consider that some of the documentation may be outdated. Some areas will have very little or no documentation and those cases require you to build it. Don't panic. This is another opportunity for you. There is no better way to learn than by building the documentation yourself. Get yourself some good partners—associates you can consult with about the environment or the company. They can be peers or engineers on your team. If your efforts take you beyond the 90—day estimate, it's alright. It's far more important to learn accurately. Seek help from your staff or from a service provider. You must tread lightly with outside help, as outside help can be perceived as a weakness by your staff, or they may decide they don't trust you because you don't feel confident that they can provide what you need. Building trust is of the utmost importance, especially in these early stages, and you don't want to start at less than zero. Try first to leverage internal staff to establish trust and help you get familiar with your team.

Introduce yourself to your team by holding your first staff meeting on your first day. Have each person introduce themselves in a manner that reveals as much about them as possible, including work history, time with the company, positions held in the past, personal ambitions, work in progress, etc. There will be opportunities for more personal sharing. Use this opportunity to state your intentions, and demonstrate your openness and willingness to work with your team to build a successful team.

Reveal just enough of yourself so that you do not remain a mystery to your team, but not so much that prejudices can be formed. Take time to meet each individual separately in your office to get friendlier one—on—one. This is a good time to ask more personal questions about where they live, their commute, their family details, their children's interests, career ambitions, etc. Don't be afraid to scratch down a note or two. Writing down some points will be seen as a strength, as these points will be interpreted as important

[208]

enough for you to write down. Writing too much takes away from that effect, so don't spend the meeting writing everything down. Your people will think you cannot remember what they say. In their mind, this meeting is about them and their world. Their boss should share their sense of importance. You, the Manager, are actually gaining critical insight from this conversation.

Put your mind and speech in the frame of "We" and less "I". Consider your team as much more important than you. Although you are clearly the Leader, establishing yourself as a part of the team and not the Dictator is significant at this stage.

Never lie or even exaggerate the facts. You are who you are. Own your past and be proud, be humble, be respectful, be grateful. Honesty is truly the best policy. Great leaders never cheat to gain respect or get ahead.

Always be positive and show happiness, even when things are not going as well as you would like. Happiness and success are contagious.

Be empathetic towards others, always able to view the situation from the perspective of others (i.e.; compassion).

Meet with your boss to discuss and clarify expectations for you.

First 90 days SYNOPSIS:

- ✓ Smile and show respect for everyone you meet.
- ✓ Dress and act the part of Leader and team player.
- ✓ Learn about your team to integrate yourself.
- ✓ Learn and understand your environment.
- ✓ Learn about your Leaders and your peers.
- ✓ Learn the basics of the business your company is in (if you think you know it, you don't. Every company is unique).
- ✓ Meet key business leaders.
- ✓ Introduce yourself to incumbent vendors.
- ✓ Document everything you learn for future reference.

This list is purposefully not numbered so you do not attempt to execute items in any order. Ideally, all items should be occurring concurrently.

Chapter 25

Getting Out Is Important to Your Success

Do not plan on hiding in your office, or even in your building. Getting out into the field occasionally, and getting exposure, will boost your respect and improve your understanding of both the work environment and of the business customer.

Has your education of the business led you to see technology opportunities for branch offices? How about for sales—process improvements? Take a trip out to a branch office. Spend time with a company sales manager and try to experience their world.

For example:
While building a data network in a new Distribution Center, my network team began to experience problems with communications to the conveyor-belt processor/bar-code reader. Our cabling vendor, through testing, determined that the problems were related to EMF (Electro-Magnetic Frequency) interference from the conveyor.

[211]

The solution was obvious. The decision could have been made from my office. Instead, I got into my car and made the two hour—long trek out to the Distribution Center (DC). I took one of my network engineers with me. We met the DC Manager, met the vendor's Project Manager, and we met the testers and installers. I physically reviewed the environment in question. After all, I was the "guy in charge" of the IT infrastructure and the final word on design details. All eyes looked to me to solve this issue. What kind of decision maker would I be if I never got out observing the environment and understanding the consequences of my decisions — if I never got out for meeting the teams and hearing their opinions?

In this instance, we were using UTP (Unshielded Twisted Pair) cable for FDX (Full Duplex) Ethernet. We could have used Shielded Twisted-Pair copper cable, but that solution came with a risk of failure. For a few dollars more, we had the talent available, and could easily get the hardware required to run fiber-optic cable to this station. This solved the problem. My site visit gave me "real" exposure to the environment, an understanding of the issues, and the respect due a decision maker who decides from a strong point of "real" experience — not someone who makes decisions from an ivory tower. Nobody noticed the few extra dollars that were spent because we delivered a reliable service over fiber optics. After operation commenced, nothing more was ever said about it. Success!

That is just one example. There were many more. Be seen and build respect. Show your successes, and show why you are successful. Field trips can be fun. When I have visited remote staff or business people, I returned to my office with new knowledge and a newfound respect for the field worker. I felt rejuvenated and energized, like I was rebooted.

Other outside activities could include industry functions such as trade shows. They seem like a real inconvenience at first, but once you arrive and meet friends and associates (maybe for the first time), you begin to feel the pressure subside. You relax and get comfortable.

Talk about what they feel is important work. Discuss personal matters. Smile, laugh, relax, have fun. This is casual networking. The people you interact with will be far more important than the sessions you attend. You can develop lasting friendships and build upon your professional network. You may not see them for another year or more, but electronic dialogue should continue regularly.

Your goal is to learn, but you should take this opportunity to share your own thoughts and accomplishments. This can be informal over coffee or lunch or formal though a presentation session with several industry peers. The latter should be considered *give—back* to your industry. Volunteer and suggest it to event organizers. It is very unlikely they will reject the idea. If the event cannot accommodate your request, you will be remembered for next time, when you may be invited to speak.

You will likely return to your office relaxed with fresh ideas and a renewed vitality. At the very least, you have made yourself known in the industry and a powerful, positive impression will pay off at some later date.

[213]

As with trade shows, industry associations can also be seen as either an inconvenience or an opportunity. You should view them as opportunities to meet peers in your industry and to learn which technologies they are using, or thinking about, for the benefit of their business. Their company's business environment is probably not too dissimilar from your company's.

I had the opportunity to share my business-networking ideas with executive members of the National Retail Federation (NRF), earning me some recognition and respect in the Retail industry. This can be considered *give-back* to your industry. This is recognition that could provide some benefit to you later in your career if you can provide value to peers. At the very least, you will be expanding your network so make it a good impression.

I caution you not to be too bold, presumptuous, or arrogant. This is not the time or place to boast. There is a danger you will alienate yourself. Peers may not wish to hear what you want to tell them. In those cases, silence is best. Listen and learn. You can still build solid, positive relationships, and not alienate anyone. You will have a mis-step now and then, but you can't make an omelet without breaking a few eggs. Smile and move on.

The most important lesson to be learned here is that you must get out and gain experience; using the knowledge you obtain to improve the business through the use of technology. You must continuously add value. You limit yourself and the value you can bring by not getting out into the world.

Chapter 26

Getting Wealthy in the Process

Try not to become a man of success but a man of value.

—Albert Einstein

Do not make monetary compensation your goal and focus. Love your work and compensation will follow.

Suggested behavior guidelines:

- Love your profession. Enjoy your job.
- Always be positive and optimistic. Opportunity is everywhere.
- Respect to be respected.
- Be prepared.
- Be efficient. Dot your i's and cross your t's.
- Seek continuous improvement.
- Be confident and firm, but humble, compassionate, and grateful.
- Dress for success.
- Communicate!

Follow these guidelines and, in time, you will achieve a respectable reputation, likeability, and esteem from company leadership. Your team will enjoy their work that much more, and others will want to join your team.

Nothing can stop the man with the right mental attitude from achieving his goal; nothing on earth can help the man with the wrong mental attitude.

—Thomas Jefferson

Take things slowly. Nothing of great and lasting value ever comes quickly or easily. Once success begins to occur regularly and you begin building a respectable reputation, compensation will come. So block it from your mind for now. Prove yourself again and again, and the money will come.

Speak with your boss and establish a relationship early (within ninety days) about your approach or your plans. Learn and understand your boss's expectations for you.

To climb steep hills requires a slow pace at first.

—Shakespeare

Demonstrate your value first.

Closing

I have found great success and enjoyment practicing these methods. Most of all, I have found great joy and fulfillment working with the good people I have shared my time and efforts with. I trust they feel the same about the time they shared with me.

This writing attempts to be non-specific about technologies. As technology evolves at an ever quickening pace, its relevance and relationship to management and leadership lessons provided in this writing should have minimal impact, so these lessons remain current. The environment will change and the nature of IT service providers will evolve, but people will still be people and leaders will still be required.

Remember that leadership is a privilege. I sincerely hope this text is of value to my IT friends and future Leaders.

The difference between a successful person and others is not a lack of strength, not a lack of knowledge, but rather a lack of will.

—Vince Lombardi

Henry Ford once said, "Whether you think you can or think you can't, you're right." Have confidence, and know that you can.

[217]

I could not, being completely truthful to my character, end my book about managing technology without an appropriate Star Trek quote:

Act, and you shall have dinner; wait, and you shall be dinner.
— Klingon proverb, Star Trek: Deep Space Nine

Manage, lead, and have fun doing it!

Best wishes,
Tim

Timothy R. Loftus, IT Manager and Infrastructure Architect, Free Knowledge Network, LLC
Website: http://www.freeknowledgenetwork.com

17 SUCCESS STRATEGIES

1. Understand your place, your role and your responsibilities.
2. Presentation: Dress for success; speak and listen professionally; write intelligently.
3. Respect to be respected.
4. Demonstrate apathy.
5. Know your environment, know your team.
6. Take care of the people that take care of you.
7. Pragmatism, honesty, courage and good sense.
8. Organize and build procedures.
9. Embrace change, searching for opportunities exposed by change.
10. Contribute to the best of your ability and do not fear hard work.
11. Be a friendly mentor and receive mentoring openly.
12. Be charitable and sympathetic, but remain stern and transparent.
13. Plan, plan, plan.
14. Move amongst your team, your offices and your businesses.
15. Promote your team and accomplishments.
16. Appreciate and give thanks.
17. Provide value and continuous improvement; opportunities abound.

Appendix A

Recommended Reading

❖ *No endorsements were received for any of the books recommended here.*

Albom, Mitch. *The Five People You Meet in Heaven.* Hyperion: New York, 2003.

Carnegie, Dale. *How to Win Friends and Influence People.* Simon and Schuster: New York, 1989.

Carnegie, Dale. *How to Stop Worrying and Start Living.* Simon and Schuster: New York, 1984.

Covey, Stephen. *The 7 Habits of Highly Effective People.* Free Press, a Division of Simon and Schuster: New York, 1989.

Giles, Lionel. *Sun Tzu on the Art of War.* Oxford University Press: London, UK, 1963.

Goldratt, Eliyahu M. *The Goal: A Process of Ongoing Improvement.* North River Press Publishing: Great Barrington, MA, 2004.

Hamilton, Scott. *The Great Eight: How to Be Happy (even when you have every reason to be miserable).* Thomas Nelson, Inc.: Nashville, TN, 2008.

Huntsman, Jon M. *Winners Never Cheat: Even in Difficult Times.* Pearson Education Inc., publishing as Prentice Hall: Upper Saddle River, NJ, 2011.

Meyer, Joyce. *A Leader in the Making: Essentials to Being a Leader after God's Own Heart.* Warner Books, Inc.: New York, 2001.

Robbins, Anthony. *Awaken the Giant Within: How to Take Immediate Control of Your Mental, Emotional, Physical and Financial Destiny!.* Free Press, a Division of Simon Schuster: New York, 1991.

Appendix B

Credits for Quotations

Scripture quotations: "Holy Bible, King James Version. Old & New Testaments [Kindle Edition]", Tony Sullivan Ministries: 2009

Serenity Prayer retrieved May 16, 2011 from
http://www.cptryon.org/prayer/special/serenity.html

Historical Leadership quotations retrieved January—May, 2011 from http://www.brainyquote.com/quotes

Other Inspirational and Leadership quotations retrieved January—May, 2011 from http://www.pickthebrain.com, http://blog.inspirationalspark.com, http://thinkexist.com

Quotations from "Apollo 13": Universal Pictures: 1995, retrieved May, 2011 from
http://www.reelmovienews.com/quotes/movies/apollo—13/

Quotation from "Star Trek": Paramount Television: 1999, John Petrie's Collection of Star Trek Quotes retrieved June, 2011from http://jpetrie.myweb.uga.edu/startrek.html

Appendix C

About the Author

Timothy R. Loftus has enjoyed thirty years in the Information Technology (IT) field, and is a certified, award—winning Leader & Managing IT Architect.

Mr. Loftus knows the IT field. Beginning after college with mainframe operations, programming and networking, advancing into PC communications (LANs/WANs, Hubs, Routers, & Switches) as well as TDM voice communications in the 1980s as a technician and a Project Manager. He managed a global IT infrastructure in the 1990s, and has more than seven years invested as an IT Architect for IBM Global Services in the 2000s where he experienced rare glimpses into many Fortune—500 IT infrastructures and support teams. Mr. Loftus has attended leadership classes and received certification from Dale Carnegie Associates, most recently becoming certified in *Converged Network Design* and educated in *ITILv3 Foundation*.

Today Mr. Loftus is a results—oriented Technology Services Management Consultant with extensive experience in managing people and processes in the design, implementation, and operation of IT infrastructures. He has demonstrated his ability to lead diverse groups of people, combining general management expertise with proven IT architecture skills and innovative technical project leadership, offering creative problem—solving analysis to improve processes and exceed goals. Mr. Loftus makes effective use of technology to empower businesses.

Learned, developed and proven skills include:
- Building Collaborative Partnerships
- IT Management, Leadership & Mentoring
- Strategic Enterprise Architecture, Planning, Deployment, Delivery & Operation
- Cloud Architecture
- Creatively utilizing technology to enhance business
- Project Management and large scale Program Management
- IT Asset Management
- ITIL Process Development and Coordination
- Budgeting and Financial Accountability
- Disaster Preparedness and Recovery

Website: http://www.freeknowledgenetwork.com

Cut out and display as a reminder for you

Cut out and utilize this "OPPORTUNITY" book mark

www.ingramcontent.com/pod-product-compliance
Lightning Source LLC
Chambersburg PA
CBHW071422050326
40689CB00010B/1944